Social Education

Text and Coursework Book for
Leaving Certificate Applied

2nd Edition

Eilis Flood

Gill & Macmillan

Gill & Macmillan Ltd
Hume Avenue, Park West, Dublin 12
with associated companies throughout the world
www.gillmacmillan.ie

© Eilis Flood 2001, 2005
0 7171 3855 0
Illustrations by Keith Barrett (maps)
and Norma Leen
Print origination in Ireland by TypeIT, Dublin

*The paper used in this book is made from the wood pulp of managed forests. For
every tree felled, at least one tree is planted, thereby renewing natural resources.*

Picture Credits:

For permission to reproduce photographs and other material, the author and publisher gratefully
acknowledge the following:

7, 53R © Rex Features; 11 © Corbis/Hulton-Deutsch Collection; SCIENCE PHOTO LIBRARY: 29T
© Conor Caffrey, 51 © Maximilian Stock Ltd, 67 © Scott Camazine/Sue Trainor, 68T
© Dr Gary Gaugler, 68B © NIBSC; 29B, 31, 62, 95, 97, 161 © Alamy Images; 42 © The Advertising
Archive; 53L © PA/Empics; 99, 214 © Irish Image Collection; 101 © Inpho; 127 © Topfoto/Scott-
Taggart; 132 © Panos Pictures/Paul Smith; 139 © Derek Speirs; 205 courtesy of the ISPCC
(www.ispcc.ie); 216 © Photocall Ireland; 264 courtesy of AIB.

For permission to reproduce logos, grateful acknowledgement is made to the following: Amnesty
International Irish Section, Department of Social and Family Affairs, St Vincent de Paul, Simon
Community, Pavee Point, CURA, CURI, Trocaire, Fianna Fail, Green Party, Labour Party, Fine Gael,
Progressive Democrats, and Sinn Fein.

The author and publisher have made every effort to trace all copyright holders, but if any has
been inadvertently overlooked we would be pleased to make the necessary arrangements
at the first opportunity.

Acknowledgments
The map extract is reprinted by permission of the Ordnance Survey of Ireland
and the Automobile Association.

Contents

Past Examinations

The teacher's CDs which accompany this book contain the following material from past examinations for the **Social Education** course:

Track 25: 2003 exam Part 1
Track 26: 2003 exam Part 2
Track 27: 2004 exam Part 1
Track 28: 2004 exam Part 2

Introduction to the Course

It is very important when we start something new that we set goals for ourselves. This means that we should think about why we are doing the new thing and what we hope to gain through doing it. What you are starting here is a totally new subject, which none of you will have studied before. Therefore, before considering your goals, find out some basic information about this course:

Activity

- What is the name of this subject? _____
- How many modules are there in the course? _____
- What is each module called?

_____

_____

_____

_____

_____

_____

When you complete each Social Education module successfully you can claim one credit. What do you need to do to claim your credit at the end of each module? The first answer has been done for you, and you have been given a clue to the others.

1. I must take part as best I can in all class activities.

2. (Something about key assignments ...) I must . . .

_____

_____

_____

3. (Something about attendance ...) I must . . .

_____

_____

_____

Module 1

Social and Health Education 1

This module should be completed during sessions 1 and 2 (Year 1) of the LCA Social Education Course.

Below are the four key assignments for Module 1. You must do ALL of them. As you work through this module and complete each assignment, come back to this page and tick it off.

1. I completed exercises and work sheets on assertive, aggressive and passive behaviour and different communication styles.

    Date: _____

2. I collected information on healthy lifestyles and made a plan to improve one aspect of my own lifestyle.

    Date: _____

3. As a member of a small group, I collected information from magazines and newspapers and used it to make a collage illustrating ways in which the media promote sex-stereotyping.

    Date: _____

4. I presented a report on a drug in which I described five things that I learned about the drug, its effects and the risks involved in taking it.

    Date: _____

Unit 1 *Self and Others*

Listening Skills

Have you ever found yourself talking to someone and getting the feeling that they were not listening? How did you know that they were not listening? How did it make you feel? We need to listen to people when they talk to us for a number of reasons. Two of these are:

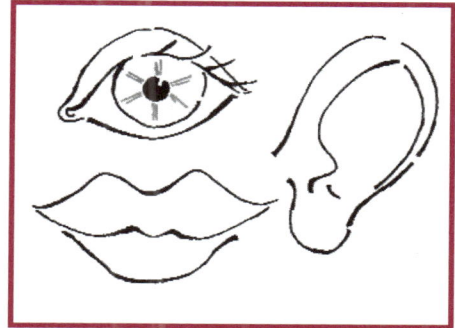

- it is polite to listen to people;
- we can get the information we need if we listen.

Effective communication

Effective communication occurs when a message of some sort is passed between two or more people. Speech may or may not be part of effective communication. Active listening is part of effective communication. The rules of active listening are as follows:

- Speak clearly.
- Keep good eye contact, both when you are speaking and when you are listening to others.
- Do not interrupt except to ask questions or if you want more information or do not fully understand.
- Sometimes we nod or say things like 'yes' or 'right', which shows we are listening.

Track 1

On Track 1 you will hear five different new stories. Listen carefully to them and then answer the questions that follow.

News story 1
1. What problem does Mr. McNamara see with the new housing developments currently being built throughout the country?

_____

_____

2. What is Mr. McNamara going to do if the government doesn't act on the problem?

_____

News story 2
1. Where exactly did the accident occur?

_____

2. Why haven't the dead men been publicly named?

_____

News story 3
1. There was no one injured in the attack on the restaurant in Clonmel. What phrase mentioned in the piece indicates this fact?

_____

2. Who owns the restaurant?

_____

News story 4
1. Where was the body found?

_____

2. Describe the dead man and his clothes.

_____

_____

3. Those with information should contact:

_____

News story 5
1. Name the four specialist units that are to be included in the new hospital.
(1) _____ (2) _____
(3) _____ (4) _____

2. What comment did local politicians make regarding the new hospital?

_____

_____

Listening to others is one way of making a class a success. Can you think of any others? Fill them in on the contract below and sign it if you mean to keep it.

Contract

In order to make Social Education a class that I enjoy, I promise to observe the following code of behaviour:

1. _____
2. _____
3. _____
4. _____
5. _____

Signed _____

Date _____

Me! I am a Positive Person

Activity

Create a collage which illustrates your long-term goals for the future. You could call your collage 'Me in 10 years time'. Use magazine cuttings, drawings of your own, etc.

Talk about your collage with the rest of the group afterwards.

Activity

Fill out the 'work card' below with information about yourself.

My name is:
My date of birth is:
When I leave school I want to be a:
A TV programme I like is:
A film I like is:
A song I like is:
One thing I like about school/youthreach is:
One thing I like about the weekend is:
My favourite dinner is:
The thing that scares me most is:
I get nervous when:

My opinions

People who litter:
Legalisation of cannabis:
Homosexuality:

Three good things about myself are:

1.
2.
3.
If I had to name one thing that I've done that I am proud of it would be:
If I could change one thing about myself it would be:

I am an Intelligent, Capable Person!

In the past many people took a very narrow view of intelligence, seeing it only in terms of passing written exams and tests. Nowadays it is generally accepted that intelligence is much broader than this, and that there is such a thing as multiple intelligence: you may not be good at exams but instead have some other skill or ability that is of value to society. Think, for example, of soccer players, musicians, or tradespeople.

Society now values different forms of intelligence.

Activity

How good are you at the following things? (Please tick)

Activity	Excellent	Good	Not very good
Sport			
Singing			
Playing an instrument			
Painting			
Looking after children			
Talking to people			
Cooking			
Keeping myself and my surroundings tidy			
Telling jokes			
Recognising a song after only a few notes			
Guessing how long something is			
Adding in my head			

Seven intelligences

In a primary school, a ten-year-old boy is having difficulty reading a book designed for a six-year-old. When the bell rings he goes out to play football. He is easily the best player in the school: he does not even have to think about what he is going to do with the ball because he just instinctively knows. Another girl is inside trying to correct her maths homework. She tries hard at maths but never seems to be able to get it right. But she is brilliant at artwork. She can paint and draw anything you could ask for. Both of these children show clear signs of intelligence, yet neither of them might score very highly on an IQ test. Individuals like this demonstrate that there are many different types of intelligence, most of which cannot be measured by the usual tests. It is believed that there are perhaps seven different forms of intelligence:

1. *Language*	People who are good at telling or writing stories, telling jokes, or songwriting.
2. *Logic and maths*	People who can fix things, make things out of wood and metal, estimate the weight or length of something, etc.
3. *Visual and spatial thinking*	People who are good at art, sculpture, photography, fashion, interior decorating, gardening.
4. *Music*	People who can play music, sing, write music.
5. *Bodily (kinesthetic)*	People who can dance or play sports well.
6. *Intrapersonal skills*	People who have a good self-knowledge.
7. *Interpersonal skills*	People who get along well with others or have good leadership skills.

Activity

Of the seven areas, which do you feel you are strongest in? Write your answer in the star.

Passive, assertive and aggressive behaviour

Being assertive is believing that you have the right to ask for what you want and need. It is closely linked to having high self-esteem or feeling good about yourself. Not everyone finds it easy to be assertive.

Some people behave passively, and do not tell others clearly what their wants and needs are. They are afraid of making enemies and so try to please everyone.

The opposite of passive is aggressive. People who behave aggressively try to bully others into getting what they want.

Track 2

Listen to Track 2 and answer the questions. In Home Economics class, students are making Swiss rolls as part of their practical cookery class. Towards the end of class the teacher asks a student to sweep the floor, he doesn't want to. There are two roleplays. Hear how the same situation can be dealt with in different ways – with different results.

1. How did the teacher relate to Aaron in both situations?

_____
_____
_____
_____

2. Why do you think Aaron reacted differently to the teacher in the two situations?

_____
_____
_____
_____

3. Which teacher (first or second one) do you think you would co-operate best with and why?

_____
_____
_____
_____

Key Assignment: Assertive, aggressive and passive behaviour

In this activity you are given a number of sample situations, and a possible response to each one. Write in the oval space whether you think the response is passive, aggressive or assertive. (You can abbreviate to pass, agg, ass.)

Situation 1

A teacher wrongly accuses you of copying in a test.

Response: You say you didn't, and ask to speak to the teacher after class so that you can explain your case calmly and fully without the whole class listening.

Situation 2 ⬭

You have bought a new outfit that you really like. Some of the others in your class make fun of it, saying it's something their mother would wear.

Response: You are confident about how the outfit looks and say that it would be a pity if we all had the same taste; the world would be a very boring place.

Situation 3 ⬭

You are in a fast food restaurant and order a burger and chips. When the food eventually comes it is cold and very greasy.

Response: You do nothing and throw the burger and chips away without eating them.

In each of the above situations, write down what you think your usual response would be, and whether you consider this response to be passive, assertive or aggressive.

Situation 1: _____

_____

Situation 2: _____

_____

Situation 3: _____

_____

Roleplays

Divide into pairs and each pair picks one of the above situations. Think about what the assertive response would be. If you like, practise roleplaying this response and then come back and present it to the whole group.

Exam Time

Social Education (2003) – Short questions

1. Phrases such as these are examples of which type of communication?

Get lost!

Shut up!

Assertive ☐   Aggressive ☐   Passive ☐

Social Education (2004) – Long question (part)

2. Describe how a young person might deal in an assertive way with a conflict situation.

Fight	Go Along With The Gang	Walk Away	Talk It Out
Shout Them Down	Stand Up For Yourself	Apologise	Ignore It
Say Nothing	Stay Calm	Speak Clearly and Slowly	Look Them In The Eyes
Be Confident	Stare Them Down	A Good Slap Always Works	Argue

_____

_____

Social Education (2004) – Long question (part)

3. What do you think Mahatma Gandhi is trying to tell us about resolving conflict?

The trouble with an eye for an eye is that it leaves the whole world blind.
MAHATMA GANDHI

_____

_____

_____

Unit 2 *Taking Care of Yourself*

The World Health Organisation (WHO) describes health as:

'A complete state of physical, mental and social well-being and not simply the absence of disease or infirmity.'

Activity

Discuss this definition of health in class and come up with six factors that contribute to a healthy lifestyle and therefore good health.

1. _____
2. _____
3. _____
4. _____
5. _____
6. _____

List six things that contribute to an unhealthy lifestyle and therefore bad health. Remember! Health means mental and social as well as physical well-being.

1. _____
2. _____
3. _____
4. _____
5. _____
6. _____

Stress And Its Management

What is stress?

Stress is a normal response that occurs when we experience or think we will experience difficulties in our lives. Stress is both physical and mental. Sometimes the cause of stress can be a one-off and be relatively short term, e.g. when moving house, changing schools or taking exams. Other times stress can be ongoing or long term, e.g. living with parents who are heavy drinkers or being bullied at school. Both types of stress are unpleasant and difficult to cope with, but because the second type is ongoing it can be the most damaging.

It is generally accepted that the stress response occurs in three stages.

Stage 1

The body becomes alarmed because it recognises that a situation is unpleasant.

A chemical hormone called adrenaline is released by the body. This hormone is called the 'fight or flight' hormone and was very important for the survival of our ancestors as they had to run away from wild animals and other dangers.

Stage 2

If the cause of the stress goes away, the body can restore itself to normal. This is the second stage and is called resistance.

Stage 3

If the cause of stress does not go away, however, the body stays in an alarmed state and eventually becomes exhausted. This is Stage 3.

It is when a person reaches Stage 3 that mental and physical health problems arise.

Common effects of stress on the body

Short term	Long term
• increased heartbeat	• frequent headaches
• faster breathing	• backache
• sweating	• asthma
• indigestion	• stomach ulcers
	• high blood pressure
	• reduced ability to fight disease

Common effects on mental well-being

• anxiety	• frustration and anger
• tension	• tiredness
• being easily irritated	• being depressed
• feeling bad about yourself (*low self-esteem*)	• being tearful
	• feeling unable to cope

Stressors

Activity

Things that cause stress are called 'stressors'. In today's society there are a huge number of stressors. Can you write down five things or situations that cause some amount of stress in your life?

1. _____
2. _____
3. _____
4. _____
5. _____

Stress and personality type

Have you ever noticed that some people seem to spend their lives looking stressed and others go through life as if they haven't a care in the world? It is thought that whether you get easily stressed or not depends largely on your personality type. There are basically two personality types:

Type A = gets stressed easily
Type B = doesn't get stressed easily

Type A personalities are always pushing themselves and are very competitive. They are not happy unless they are the best at whatever they decide to do. Type A personalities need frequent praise and recognition. They are always rushing against the clock and are sometimes irritable and unreasonable. They tend to suffer more from stress and stress-related illnesses.

Type B personalities on the other hand are sometimes thought of as being lazy. They do not really push themselves and rarely do more than enough to get through. They are not very competitive and do not get upset if others achieve more than they do. Type B personalities like praise but do not go looking for it. They avoid confrontation with others at all costs.

Note: Type A and B are fairly extreme; many people fall somewhere in between the two personality types.

What personality type are you?

1. Does it annoy you when a teacher is slow
to give back corrected work?   Yes ☐   No ☐

2. Would you know what mark others in
your class got in a test?   Yes ☐   No ☐

3. Would you borrow money to buy brand
name clothes?   Yes ☐   No ☐

4. Generally do you walk quickly?   Yes ☐   No ☐

5. Do you often eat while standing up?   Yes ☐   No ☐

6. Are you often late for things?   Yes ☐   No ☐

7. If a friend wanted to go out and you
didn't, would you go anyway?   Yes ☐   No ☐

8. Do you find it difficult to sit still in class? Yes ☐   No ☐

9. When you are eating a packet of sweets
do you chew more than one at a time?   Yes ☐   No ☐

10. When you are getting ready to go out
do you try on several outfits before
choosing what to wear?   Yes ☐   No ☐

11. Do you get heartburn frequently?   Yes ☐   No ☐

12. Do you get headaches frequently?   Yes ☐   No ☐

13. Do you get very nervous before a test?   Yes ☐   No ☐

14. Do you fidget a lot?   Yes ☐   No ☐

15. Do you bite your nails?   Yes ☐   No ☐

Count the number of yes and no answers you had. Write the
results below.

Yes answers _____   No answers _____

If you had 10-15 'yes' answers you seem to have a 'type A' personality. If you had 10-15 'no' answers then you seem to have a 'type B' personality. If you have roughly 7-8 of each you are in between.

People need a certain amount of stress to stay alert and interested in their lives. If we are under-stressed we will not be enthusiastic in our work, be frequently bored or even depressed.

Stress management

Stress is an unfortunate but unavoidable part of modern life. Stress as we have already seen is very dangerous if it is not managed properly. Some people manage their stress very badly or not at all. They:

- overeat;
- drink too much;
- smoke too much;
- take drugs;
- avoid going to work or school if this is where the stress is;
- stay out late if the stress is at home.

People who try to cope with stress in these ways eventually exhaust themselves and burn out. Luckily there are other, much better ways of dealing with stress in our lives.

The first step to good stress management is to accept that there is a problem or are problems in your life that are causing you stress. You must then decide what to do with them.

You have two basic choices:

1. Try to get rid of the cause of the stress (the problem).
2. Try to cope effectively with the symptoms of stress.

Take this example:

Some people in your class will not sit beside you because they say you smell. This causes you stress.

What can you do? You can get rid of the problem by washing your clothes and yourself every day.

However, not all problems can be solved like this. Take this example:

You have come to live in Ireland from England and have to study Irish as part of your LCA. You get very stressed when you have Irish class as it is too difficult and everyone knows more than you. You cannot avoid the problem, i.e. by missing class everyday, so you must learn to deal with the problem in other ways.

Some ways of coping with stress are:

- Talking to a trusted friend about your problem.
- Exercise, e.g. walking or playing a physical game.
- Breathing or other relaxation exercises.
- OLGA – a coping mechanism.

Breathing techniques

When you feel stressed, e.g. at the start of an exam, try this breathing technique.

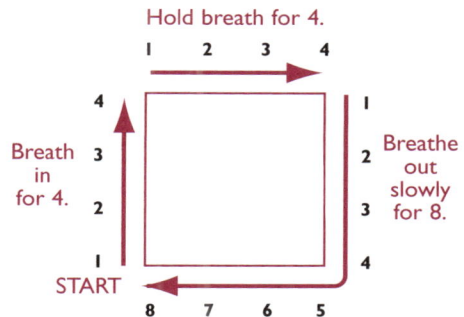

Hold breath for 4.

Breath in for 4.

Breathe out slowly for 8.

START

Track 3	**Relaxation exercise**
	Listen to Track 3 and carry out the relaxation exercise as you listen.

Activity	**OLGA**
	OLGA is a way of dealing with stress in three simple stages: **Stage 1 – O** OBSERVE what is happening to you. For example, you think your boyfriend or girlfriend is seeing someone else behind your back. You are in class thinking about this and it is driving you mad and causing you a lot of stress. **Stage 2 – LG** LET GO - there is nothing you can do about it at this point in time. **Stage 3 – A** ATTEND – to what you are meant to be doing. Put the thoughts of your boyfriend or girlfriend away and concentrate on what you should be doing now, i.e. your school work.

Track 4

Listen to Track 4 and answer the questions. Fiona is 17. She is a bright young girl being bullied by a group of girls at school. The ringleader is a girl called Sonya, who is not very good at school. Sonya and her gang bully Fiona in a very subtle, yet cruel way. Fiona has started to miss school regularly because of it. Her year head, Ms Browne, has noticed this and talks to Fiona about it.

1. What causes Fiona to experience stress?

_____

_____

2. Sonya and her gang bully Fiona in a very subtle, yet cruel way. What do you think this means?

_____

_____

3. Why do you think people bully?

_____

_____

4. How does Fiona try to cope with the stress?

_____

_____

5. Is her stress management effective? If not, what could she do instead?

_____

_____

Good Nutrition

Healthy eating is very important for you to look well and feel well. No face creams or health supplements can take the place of eating a wide variety of fresh foods and drinking plenty of fresh clean water. Most of us have some idea of what we should and should not be eating, but for a lot of people working out a balanced diet for themselves seems all too complicated and too much like hard work! The food pyramid opposite is designed to take the hard work out of planning a healthy, balanced diet for a teenager.

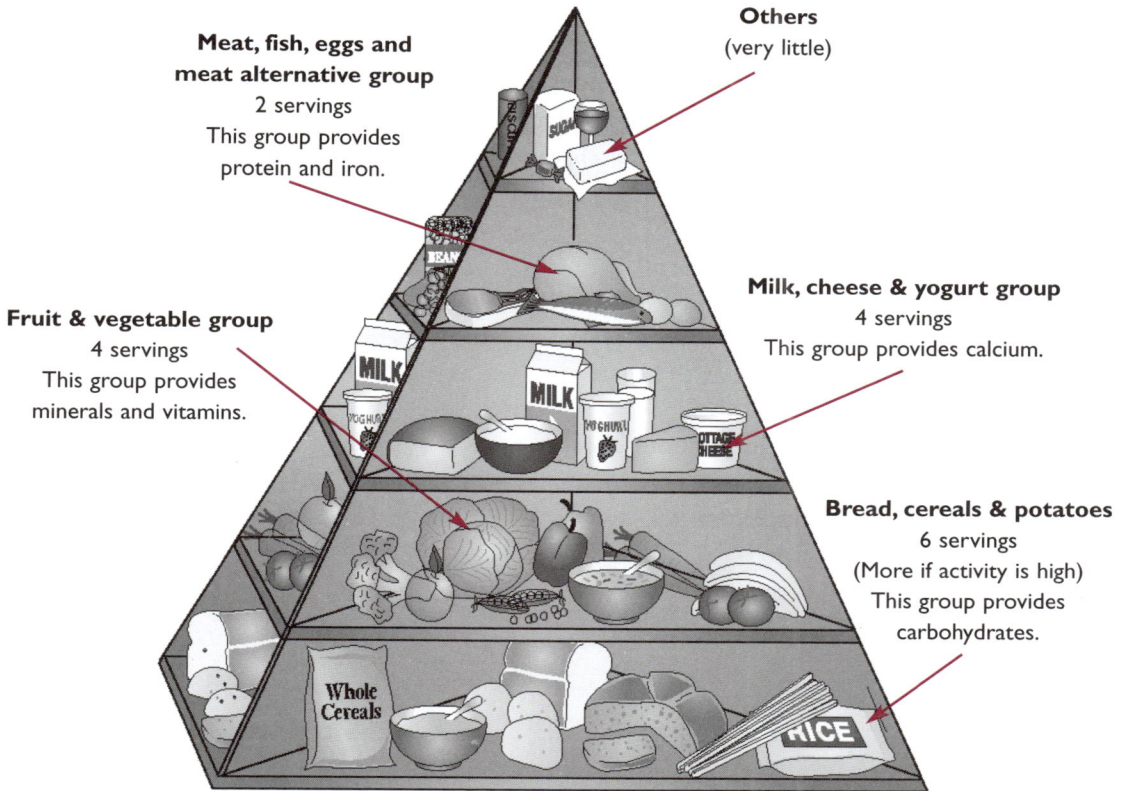

Others (very little)

Meat, fish, eggs and meat alternative group
2 servings
This group provides protein and iron.

Milk, cheese & yogurt group
4 servings
This group provides calcium.

Fruit & vegetable group
4 servings
This group provides minerals and vitamins.

Bread, cereals & potatoes
6 servings
(More if activity is high)
This group provides carbohydrates.

What is a serving?

Bread, cereals & potato group	Fruit and vegetable group	Milk, cheese and yoghurt group	Meat, fish, eggs and meat alternative group
1 bowl of cereal, 1 slice of bread, 4 dessertspoons of rice/pasta, 1 potato.	½ glass fruit juice, 4 dessertspoons cooked vegetables, 1 bowl homemade vegetable soup, 1 piece fresh fruit, 4 dessertspoons of cooked or tinned fruit.	1 glass milk, 1 carton yoghurt, 1 matchbox-sized piece of cheese.	50g red meat/chicken, 75g fish, 2 eggs, 12 dessertspoons peas/beans, 75g nuts, 75g TVP.

If a person has trouble with their diet, for example they are very over or under weight, they can go to the hospital to see a dietitian. The dietitian would try to get an idea of what sort of eating habits the person has by doing a 24-hour recall. This means that the dietitian finds out and writes down exactly what the person eats and drinks in a given 24-hour period. Below is a 24-hour recall chart for you to fill out. It is not as complicated as a real one but it will give you a general picture of your eating habits none the less.

Activity

24-hour recall

What did you eat yesterday? Write down everything, including sweets, drinks, etc. Be as accurate as you can, for example write 'two slices of bread', not just 'bread'.

Date of 24-hour recall _____

Breakfast	Mid-morning break
Lunch	Mid-afternoon break
Dinner	Supper

Evaluate your eating habits:

In general do you think your diet is a healthy one?

Yes ☐   No ☐

What foods should you increase? _____

_____

What foods should you reduce? _____

_____

Using the knowledge that you have gained as a result of studying the food pyramid, plan out a daily menu for yourself.

(This activity will fulfil the first part of your Key Assignment 2.) When you have completed the second part of this key assignment, go to the beginning of this module and tick it off on the checklist.

Daily Menu

Breakfast:

Mid-morning break:

Lunch:

Mid-afternoon break:

Evening dinner:

Supper:

Safe Alcohol Limits

Fully grown men 21 units per week (no more than 6-8 in one night)
Fully grown women 14 units per week (no more than 4-6 in one night)

I unit	2 units	I unit	I ¹/₂ units	I unit
Glass of lager, cider, beer	Pint of lager, cider, beer	Glass of wine	Ready-mixed drink (Alcopop)	Shot of spirits

Activity

What is a unit?

1. On Sunday night Peter drank 5 pints and a vodka and coke.

How many units did he consume? _____

Is he within recommended limits?   Yes ☐   No ☐

2. On Saturday night Eoin drank 3 pints of cider.

How many units did he consume? _____

Is he within recommended limits?   Yes ☐   No ☐

3. On Monday night Samantha drank 4 glasses of lager.

How many units did she consume? _____

Is she within recommended limits?   Yes ☐   No ☐

4. On Saturday night Anna drank 5 ready-mixed alcopops.

How many units did she consume? _____

Is she within recommended limits?   Yes ☐   No ☐

Exercise and Fitness

Exercise, like eating well, is something that is very important if we are to feel and look good. Young children don't need to be told to take exercise. It is usually when children turn into young adults that some may stop taking regular exercise. During the teenage years patterns are established that may stay with you for life. This is why it is important to take regular exercise when you go into secondary school and keep it up even when you leave school.

Activity

Below are a list of reasons why people take regular exercise.
Tick whether each reason is important to you or not.

To keep fit	Yes ☐	No ☐
To look well	Yes ☐	No ☐
To meet lots of people	Yes ☐	No ☐
To build up and keep good bone density	Yes ☐	No ☐
I like it.	Yes ☐	No ☐
To release stress	Yes ☐	No ☐
To prevent heart disease	Yes ☐	No ☐

To keep my lungs healthy and strong	Yes ☐	No ☐
To keep my weight down	Yes ☐	No ☐
I like winning.	Yes ☐	No ☐
Sport is my talent.	Yes ☐	No ☐

Activity

Survey of exercise habits

Why not find out how much exercise others in your school or centre take each week. You could do this by getting them to fill out a questionnaire like the one below. When you have the questionnaires filled out, present your results using bar charts, etc.

Regular exercise questionnaire

1. Are you male or female? _____

2. Approximately how much free time did you have in the last 24 hours? _____

3. Which of these activities do you do most in your free time? (pick one)

A. Watch TV or videos	☐	E. Listen to music	☐
B. Computer games	☐	F. Sleep	☐
C. Read books/magazines	☐	G. Play sports	☐
D. Go into town with friends	☐	H. Meet my boy/girlfriend	☐

4. Would you describe yourself as a physically active individual?

Yes ☐   No ☐

5. Tick the exercise you take most often. How often you take part in this activity, e.g. twice a week, etc.

A. Walking	☐ _____	E. Basketball	☐ _____
B. Football	☐ _____	F. Camogie	☐ _____
C. Jogging	☐ _____	G. Dancing	☐ _____
D. Swimming	☐ _____	H. Other	☐ _____

6. Do you think that exercise is important?   Yes ☐   No ☐

7. Tick any of the reasons below that are important to you.

A. It keeps my heart and lungs healthy. ☐
B. It keeps my weight down. ☐
C. It keeps me out of trouble. ☐
D. I would be bored if I didn't
   take exercise. ☐
E. I meet people through
   sport/exercise. ☐
F. I enjoy it. ☐
G. Sport is my best talent. ☐

Get Fit! – Make the Effort
Name one physical activity that you will participate in next week.

_____

Rest, Relaxation and Sleep

Rest, relaxation and sleep are vital to good health as this is how the body re-energises itself. It is recommended that you get at least eight hours' sleep every night.

Activity

Starting next Monday, monitor the number of hours' sleep you get for the whole week and record your findings below. Add all the hours together and divide by 7 to get the average number of hours' sleep that you had per night.

Monday night	_____	Tuesday night	_____
Wednesday night	_____	Thursday night	_____
Friday night	_____	Saturday night	_____
Sunday night	_____		

Average per night _____

Psychological Well-Being

Psychological or mental well-being is another essential ingredient for good health. The following are necessary to achieve this. Discuss what each one means with your teacher and the rest of the group.

- positive self image;
- a sense of belonging;
- a sense of security and safety;
- fun and enjoyment.

Drugs

What is a drug?

A drug is a substance (with the exception of food) that changes:

- how the body works;
- how a person acts;
- how a person feels;
- how a person thinks.

Classification of drugs

There are five main categories of drugs.

Category	General effects	Examples
Sedatives	Relief of tension/anxiety. Sleep-inducing. Physical and psychological dependence.	Sleeping tablets, tranquillisers e.g. Valium, cannabis.
Hallucinogens	Causes changes in mood and thought patterns. May see/hear things not really there. Bad trips, flashbacks.	LSD, magic mushrooms, Ecstasy, cannabis.
Depressants	Slow down nervous system, making person more relaxed but co-ordination affected.	Alcohol.
Opiates	Cause feelings of euphoria but physically and psychologically addictive.	Heroin, methadone, morphine.
Stimulants	Increase heart and breathing rates. Prevents sleep. Fluid loss.	Caffeine, nicotine, Ecstasy, cocaine.

Most countries try to stop dangerous drug use by banning or limiting their use. Countries do this for the following reasons:
- health promotion (e.g. government warning on cigarettes);
- protection of others (e.g. drink driving laws);
- keeping law and order (e.g. to stop addicts stealing to feed their habits).

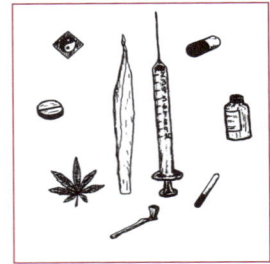

Activity

1. List all the reasons you can think of for a young person deciding to get involved in drugs.

_____

_____

_____

2. List all the reasons you can think of for a young person deciding not to get involved in drugs.

_____

_____

_____

3. 'Frequently drug addicts blame things like coming from a bad area, unemployment and family problems for getting involved with drugs in the first place. Some people think it is time they stopped blaming everyone else and started taking responsibility for their own behaviour.'

Discuss this statement with your class group. Write down what you think below.

_____

_____

_____

Smoking

Over the years many thousands of euros have been spent by the Government in an effort to stop people smoking. Some people think that this money has been largely wasted, believing that there are as many people smoking today as ever. It is now illegal to buy cigarettes under 18 years of age.

Activity

Your group could carry out a piece of research on smoking in your school/centre by asking other classes to fill out this or a similar smoking questionnaire. Present your results using pie charts, bar charts, etc.

Smoking questionnaire

1. Are you: Male ☐   Female ☐
2. Are you over 18?   Yes ☐   No ☐
3. Do you smoke?   Yes ☐   No ☐

If yes, on average how many cigarettes do you smoke per day?
0-5 ☐   5-10 ☐   10-15 ☐   15-20 ☐   more ☐

4. Do you know how much a packet of cigarettes costs?

                                             Yes ☐   No ☐

If yes, how much? _____

5. Why do you smoke? You can tick more than one.
(Leave blank if you do not smoke.)
A. Cigarettes make me feel more confident.   ☐
B. Smoking calms me.   ☐
C. All my friends smoke.   ☐
D. I am addicted.   ☐
F. No good reason.   ☐

6. Attitudes to smoking – what do you think?

	Agree	Don't know	Disagree
A. The bad effects of smoking are exaggerated.	☐	☐	☐
B. Smoking is a filthy habit.	☐	☐	☐
C. Quitting smoking is very difficult.	☐	☐	☐
D. Banning smoking in all public places is a good thing.	☐	☐	☐
E. Smoking has a glamorous image.	☐	☐	☐
F. Smoking will affect my health.	☐	☐	☐
G. It is easy to tell from their appearance if a person smokes or not.	☐	☐	☐

7. In years to come, if your children started smoking, what would you do?

_____

_____

The effects of smoking on the heart and lungs

Diseases of the lungs

Lung cancer

Approximately 90% of lung cancer victims smoke. Tar and other substances found in cigarettes cause cancer cells to form in the lungs. Non-smokers (passive smokers) who spend a lot of time in the company of smokers are also at risk.

Bronchitis

Continuous smoking causes the tubes and the air sacs of the lungs to become filled with mucus or phlegm. The person tries to get rid of the phlegm by coughing it up; this is the 'smoker's cough'. Eventually the tubes and the air sacs become infected and the person goes down with bronchitis. The symptoms of bronchitis are fever, severe coughing and a feeling of not being able to get your breath. Permanent damage occurs when the air sacs become so choked that they become destroyed, leaving the person with permanent breathing difficulties. Bronchitis is the most common disease among smokers.

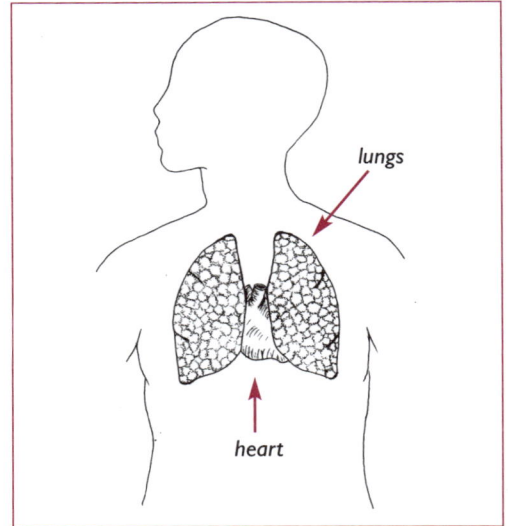

Emphysema

Emphysema is a very serious incurable disease of the lungs. Smoking causes the lungs to become so badly damaged that they cannot function anymore. Someone with emphysema would have trouble climbing stairs or doing anything else that requires energy. Seventy-five per cent of deaths from emphysema are smoking-related.

Diseases of the heart

Heart attacks

Smoking causes the hormone adrenaline to be released into the blood steam. Adrenaline causes the heart to beat faster; over the years this puts strain on the heart. Eventually this could lead to a heart attack.

Arteriosclerosis

Smoking is one of the causes of arteriosclerosis or hardening of the arteries. This causes bad circulation which again puts strain on the heart and so increases the risk of heart failure.

Blood clots

Smoking also causes the blood to clot more easily in the blood vessels.

Passive smokers

Passive smokers, that is people who are frequently exposed to other people's smoke, in time run the same risks as actual smokers.

The effects of smoking on the rest of the body

- Strokes are usually caused when a blood clot forms in the brain. Strokes are more common in smokers than non-smokers. Strokes can give a person brain damage and leave the person paralysed or partially paralysed. Strokes are a very common cause of disability in this country.
- The skin is affected by smoking; smokers tend to get more wrinkles and age more quickly than non-smokers.
- Smoking discolours teeth and hair.
- Smoking reduces your sense of taste and smell.

Smoking causes premature ageing and discoloration of hair and teeth.

Smoking and pregnancy

If you smoke your baby smokes too.

- There is an increased risk of having a miscarriage or a stillborn baby.
- Babies of smokers are on average up to half a pound lighter than babies of non-smokers, and are more likely to be premature.
- Smoking around a baby after he or she is born increases the risk of cot death. At least 63% of babies who die from cot death had mothers who smoke. At least 64% had fathers who smoked. (Sudden Infant Death Registrar 2002).

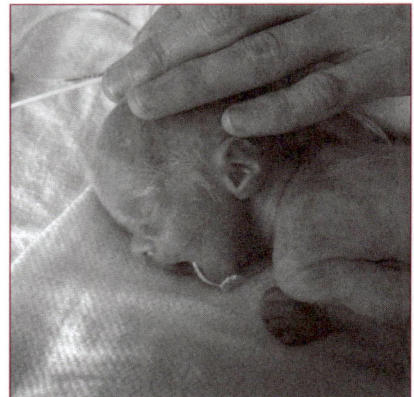

The baby of a smoker is more likely to be premature.

- Smoking around a baby before or after he or she is born increases the risk of developing diseases such as bronchitis and asthma.
- Research shows delays in the physical, emotional and intellectual development of the babies of some smokers.
- Smoking reduces fertility in both men and women.
- Smoking causes menopause to come 1-2 years early.
- Smoking is linked to cancer of the womb and the cervix (opening of the womb).

What if I give up?

If a smoker decides to give up, the news is good.

- Some people who have been smoking for years believe that it is too late because the damage is done. This is not true – the risk of dying from smoking-related diseases dramatically reduces soon after the smoker quits.

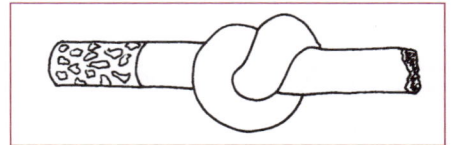

- Women who stop smoking in the first 2-3 months of pregnancy are not any more at risk of having low birth weight babies than women who did not smoke at all.

- Stopping smoking is a great achievement. It gives the smoker a sense of pride in having done something worthwhile.

- If you smoke a packet a day you can look forward to saving around €2,200 per year.

- Giving up improves the skin's appearance.

- Some people put on weight; about half a stone is usual. This weight will soon be lost again as people feel they have more energy and take more exercise.

Activity

Smoking quiz

1. What age do you have to be to legally buy cigarettes?_____

2. What is the major effect of smoking on the brain?

_____

3. Describe in your own words what bronchitis is.

_____

_____

---

4. Describe in your own words what emphysema is.

_____

_____

5. What in your opinion is the worst effect of smoking during pregnancy?

_____

_____

6. What is passive smoking?

_____

_____

Cannabis

Origin

The drug cannabis, the world's most popular illegal drug, comes from a bushy plant called *cannabis sativa*. Cannabis is grown in large quantities in South America, Africa, and Middle and Far Eastern countries such as Pakistan, Afghanistan, China, Cambodia, India and Iran. It is then smuggled from these countries to the rest of the world. Cannabis has been used as a drug for centuries, especially in China and Ancient Greece, where it was used as a medicine. Cannabis became very popular in America and Europe in the 1960s; in the 1980s its popularity declined, only to become fashionable again in the 1990s.

Cannabis takes three forms:

Cannabis herb is the leaves and flowers of the plant. It is also called marijuana, grass, dope, pot, weed, etc.

Cannabis resin is when the plant is mixed with oil or resin and compressed or squashed into blocks. This substance is called hash, hashish, blow, etc.

Cannabis oil is when the juices are taken out of the plant and distilled to make them concentrated. This form is rare in Ireland.

Cannabis comes in different forms.

What are the effects of cannabis use?

Short-term effects

- relaxation
- talkativeness
- giddiness
- feeling of slowed time
- sometimes colour, sensory and musical perception become altered

Sometimes the short-term effects may not be pleasant. Here are some common ones:

- vomiting
- headaches
- paranoia
- confusion
- fearfulness
- lack of co-ordination
- panic attacks

Cannabis impairs your ability to ride a bicycle, drive a car or do anything else that requires good co-ordination.

Long-term effects

Some people believe that cannabis should be made legal, and that it doesn't really damage the user's health. Others believe that cannabis is a very harmful drug and that it definitely should not be made legal.

Facts about cannabis

- Cannabis contains 421 different chemicals. The most important and dangerous of these chemicals is THC. THC affects the brain, reproductive systems, lungs and the immune systems of heavy cannabis users. THC clings to the fatty tissue in your body and can be detected in the urine up to a month after taking a single joint.

- Cannabis has three times more cancer-causing tar than strong cigarettes.

- Cannabis smoking over prolonged periods can cause the following:
    - lack of interest/ambition;
    - short-term memory loss;
    - reduced learning ability;
    - being absent a lot from school or work;
    - dropping out of school.

- The male sex hormone testosterone reduces by 25-30% within three hours of smoking cannabis.

- Women who smoke cannabis during pregnancy are likely to have:
    - a smaller baby;
    - a baby who has less well-defined muscles;
    - a baby who is more jittery, irritable and less attentive.

- Long-term cannabis use can trigger mental illness such as depression and schizophrenia.

- There is nothing in cannabis itself that causes people to try other illegal drugs. Even so, some research shows that cannabis users are more likely to experiment with other drugs than non-cannabis users.

- Cannabis use is illegal and if you are caught using or supplying cannabis a fine or imprisonment will result. A conviction for use or possession may damage your career prospects or hinder your ability to travel abroad.

Activity

Test yourself on the questions below.

Question 1   (Circle true or false)

A. Cannabis makes you more alert and better able to carry out tasks.   T   F

B. Cannabis produces less tar than strong cigarettes.   T   F

C. Cannabis is illegal.   T   F

D. Cannabis is a newly discovered drug.   T   F

E. Cannabis has a bad effect on the male and female reproductive systems.   T   F

F. Cannabis traces stay in the body for a number of weeks.   T   F

G. Cannabis helps you concentrate and do better at school/work.   T   F

H. The most dangerous chemical in cannabis is called THC.   T   F

I. Cannabis users are more likely to start other drugs than non-cannabis users.   T   F

J. If you are caught with cannabis you will be fined or imprisoned.   T   F

Question 2
Name three unpleasant short-term effects of cannabis use.

1. _____

2. _____

3. _____

Question 3

What do you consider to be the three most worrying long-term effects of cannabis use?

1. _____
2. _____
3. _____

Question 4

Why do you think cannabis users are more likely to use other illegal drugs?

_____
_____
_____
_____

Activity

Distribute the questionnaire below to other groups in your school or centre. Present your results using graphs, etc.

Cannabis questionnaire

1. Age:
   - 12-15 ☐
   - 16-18 ☐
   - 19 and over ☐

2. Are you: Male ☐   Female ☐

3. Please give your opinion on the following statements:

	Agree	Don't know	Disagree
A. Cannabis is a harmless drug.	☐	☐	☐
B. Cannabis should be made legal.	☐	☐	☐
C. Regular cannabis smoking can make a person less ambitious or interested in life.	☐	☐	☐
D. Cannabis use helps you concentrate.	☐	☐	☐
E. Cannabis smoking causes cancer.	☐	☐	☐

4. Have you ever smoked cannabis?   Yes ☐   No ☐

5. Do you know anyone who uses cannabis regularly?
                                       Yes ☐   No ☐

6. Would you smoke cannabis if it were offered to you?
                                       Yes ☐   No ☐

LSD

Origin

LSD was first manufactured in the 1920s although it did not come into common usage until the 1960s and early 1970s during the 'hippie' era. LSD made a comeback at the end of the 1980s and the beginning of the 1990s. Acid house music gets part of its name from LSD's full title which is lysergic acid diethylamide.

Appearance

LSD usually comes on strong paper sheets which have been dipped in the drug. Each sheet is made up of many small squares, which are torn off individually. Each square carries a logo. Common logos are bat wings, a black star, strawberries, mushrooms, a smiley face, etc.

Effects

LSD is a hallucinogenic drug which causes the user to hallucinate or become removed from reality. Sometimes hallucinations can be bad or frightening. When this happens this is called a 'bad trip'. Perhaps the most worrying effect of LSD use is that some users report having unpleasant flashbacks long after taking the drug.

Read the letter below and give your opinion in the space provided.

Dear Joan,

My name is Michael and I am 17 years old. Last weekend I went to a nightclub near where I live. I don't go out much so when I arrived and a few of the guys in my class came over I was really relieved. At least I wouldn't be standing there on my own all night. They seemed really delighted to see me. After talking to them for a while I realised they were definitely on something. I was praying they wouldn't ask me to take any, but of course they did. I didn't know what to do.

1. What pressures are there on Michael to take LSD?

_____

_____

2. If Michael takes the drug what could the consequences be?

_____

_____

3. If Michael refuses the drug what could the consequences be?

_____

_____

4. What would you do or say if you were in Michael's position?

_____

_____

The truth about Ecstasy

Origin

Ecstasy is a drug that was invented in Germany before the First World War as a slimming aid because it causes the user to become energised and therefore burn up calories. The drug was never however made legal, because it was not safe enough. Ecstasy was largely forgotten about until the 1980s and 1990s when 'house music' and 'rave' culture first became popular.

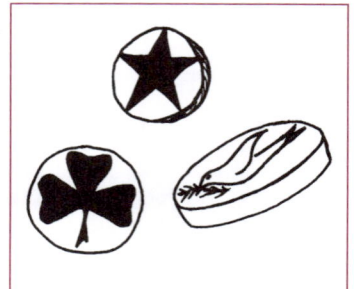

Appearance

Ecstasy or 'E' is sold under many different names; examples include 'doves' and 'shamrocks', reflected in the logo imprinted on them. Tablets are generally about the size of a paracetamol tablet. There are no official figures for Ecstasy use but it is thought that as many young people try Ecstasy as tobacco.

Short-term effects

- Blood pressure rises, the heart beats faster and the user's body temperature increases.
- The user feels relaxed and becomes friendly towards others.
- The user becomes full of energy.
- The user sweats a lot and feels thirsty.

Long-term effects

Because Ecstasy has only been popular since the 1980s, unfortunately not much is known about its long-term effects. It is thought, though, that the brain can suffer permanent damage in some cases.

Dangers!

Most people are aware that there have been a number of cases of young people dying from Ecstasy use. Dehydration is one of the main problems associated with the drug. Some nightclub owners have made money out of this problem, by turning taps off in the toilets and forcing dancers to buy water at inflated prices. Young people have suffered heart attacks, kidney failure, liver damage and heat stroke as a result of taking Ecstasy. There have been reports of others falling to their deaths because their co-ordination has been so badly impaired. Some young people have reported panic attacks and depression in the days and weeks following Ecstasy use.

Track 5

Listen to Track 5 and answer the questions.

1. How many people have died from Ecstasy use this year? _____

2. What did the post-mortem results reveal in this case?

_____

_____

3. How does the media normally portray or show drug users?

_____

_____

_____

4. What information is there in this report to show that Ecstasy use spans all social and economic groups?

_____

_____

_____

5. What does this report suggest should be done to help the problem?

_____

_____

Heroin

Origin

Heroin, like morphine, comes from the opium poppy. Pakistan and the Far East are the biggest heroin producers in the world. Heroin was used as a medicine until about three hundred years ago, when its effect on the mind became known. Heroin began to be used for non-medicinal purposes in the 1800s with the invention of the syringe.

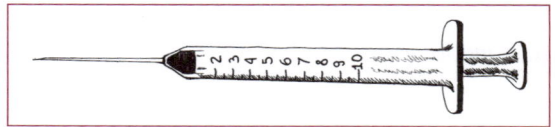

Appearance

Heroin is sold as a white or brown powder in small packets or 'deals'. Heroin sold on the street is generally diluted or 'cut'. Sometimes dealers cut heroin with substances such as talcum powder, Vim or chalk dust, which makes it very dangerous to use. Heroin is either injected, smoked or snorted and is sometimes called smack, junk or horse.

Effects of heroin use

The most widely publicised effect of heroin addiction is getting HIV and other viruses from the use of infected or 'dirty' needles. Even if a heroin addict does not contract HIV, their health frequently suffers. Heart failure, pneumonia, loss of appetite, weight loss and lung infections are common among users. Addicts sometimes overdose or unknowingly use heroin that is impure. This can result in death.

It is estimated that there are over 15,000 heroin addicts in Ireland. Unlike other drugs, which are equally popular across all the social classes, heroin use tends to be concentrated in areas of high unemployment and poverty. Ironically, heroin is one of the most expensive drugs available. It can cost over €125 per day to feed a habit. As a result some addicts resort to dealing or other crimes such as robbery to pay for their supply.

Withdrawing from heroin addiction can be very difficult. The addict may suffer bouts of diarrhoea, vomiting, headaches and the shakes. One minute the addict may feel boiling hot and the next freezing cold, and may also hallucinate. These withdrawal symptoms are called 'cold turkey'.

Activity

Answer the following questions on heroin.

1. What do you think are the three most worrying effects of heroin addiction?

_____

_____

2. What effect does heroin abuse have on society in general?

_____

_____

3. Find out what a needle-exchange programme is. What is your opinion of this kind of programme?

_____

_____

Perhaps your class could watch a film that looks at the drugs issue. *Trainspotting* is a hard-hitting film about heroin addition.

Facts about solvent abuse

Solvent abuse is the term given to the deliberate inhaling of gases or fumes from a number of commonly available substances. The main substances sniffed are:

- glue
- paint thinner
- aerosols
- fuels, gas, petrol
- dry cleaning products.

- In Ireland there are up to 10 cases of people dying from solvent abuse every year.
- Someone who has inhaled solvents appears to be drunk; they have slurred speech and stagger. Sometimes solvent abuse causes hallucinations.
- The next day the solvent abuser may have headaches, not be able to concentrate, have no appetite and suffer mood swings.
- If someone abuses solvents on a regular basis, there is usually weight loss, disturbed sleep and a characteristic rash around the user's mouth and nose.

Activity

Eoin's story

Eoin started on solvents when he was about 14 years old. Every evening he and a few friends would go up onto some waste ground near where they lived to sniff whatever substance they were able to get their hands on that day. The hardware store in their area was getting very suspicious and was starting to refuse to give any sort of solvents to young people. Eoin knew how to get around this problem. All he had to do was to go to a shop in a 'posh' area about two miles away; he never had any trouble getting solvents there.

Eoin knew that his solvent habit was having a bad effect on him, but nobody else seemed worried. His parents were too busy fighting to notice any change in him. Most of his teachers didn't really notice him either. He wasn't particularly good at school so the fact that his results were getting worse didn't seem to trouble anyone.

Can you finish the story?

_____

_____

_____

_____

_____

_____

_____

Alcohol

Attitudes and images of alcohol

Alcohol is one product that is heavily advertised on TV and in the print media. Advertisers use various techniques to convince you to buy their products. Here are some of them.

Use of a famous/glamorous/sexy person

This person will claim that he or she uses the product and finds it really good. The ad wants you to believe that if you use this product you will be sexy and glamorous too.

Can you think of one alcohol advertisement that uses this technique?

_____

_____

Humour

Can you think of one alcohol advertisement that uses this technique?

_____

_____

Use of exaggeration

An example of this: 'the best built car in the world'.

Can you think of one alcohol advertisement that uses this technique?

_____

_____

Use of slogans

An example of this is 'Live life to the power of Guinness'.

Can you think of one other alcohol advertisement that uses this technique?

_____

_____

Activity

Look at advertisements for alcoholic drinks on TV. Answer the questions about one advertisement.

Name of alcoholic drink advertised _____

1. What time did you see the ad on TV?

_____

2. During what TV programme was the ad shown?

_____

3. What advertising technique(s) were used?

_____
_____
_____

4. Who is the ad aimed at? Give a reason for your answer.

_____
_____
_____

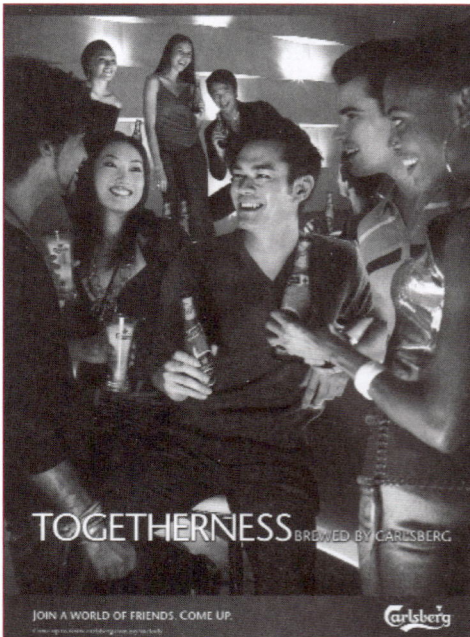

TOGETHERNESS BREWED BY CARLSBERG

JOIN A WORLD OF FRIENDS. COME UP.

Carlsberg

5. Look at this ad. What is this ad implying? If you drink this product:

_____
_____
_____
_____
_____
_____
_____
_____
_____
_____
_____

Addictions

When someone becomes either physically, socially or psychologically dependent on a substance or a behaviour they are said to be addicted to or dependent on that substance or behaviour.

Alcohol misuse or addiction

In the past people were called alcoholics if they frequently drank in excessive quantities. This term brought with it images of people down and out, begging for their next drink. In more recent times the word alcoholic has been replaced by problem drinker or alcohol misuser. This has been in an effort to have people realise that you do not have to be on the streets, drinking a bottle of cheap cider to be a problem drinker. In fact there is evidence to show that the highest level of problem drinking occurs among doctors and dentists.

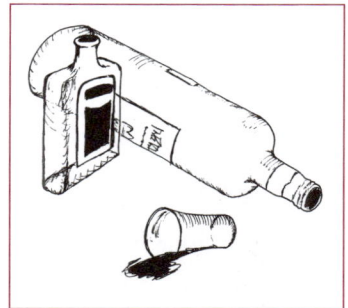

The effects of alcohol misuse on the body

The liver

Alcohol is poisonous to the body. The liver is the organ which breaks alcohol down into substances that do not harm the body. It can safely break down about one unit of alcohol per hour. If a person frequently drinks heavily, the liver cannot cope and becomes damaged. Cirrhosis of the liver is the disease that results. This disease can be fatal. Other diseases such as gout, where there is a painful swelling of the joints, usually of the toes, are common in heavy drinkers.

The stomach

Alcohol irritates the stomach and can cause ulcers, which are sores on the lining of the stomach.

The brain

Long-term misuse of alcohol can cause brain damage. If you have a blackout, brain cells are being killed that are not being replaced. If this occurs frequently, the person can become permanently brain-damaged, for example with the memory badly affected.

Other effects on the individual

If alcohol is taken in moderate amounts it causes the person to become relaxed and perhaps more sociable. If a lot of alcohol is taken, a person becomes unco-ordinated and starts to stagger. Judgement is badly affected. Studies show that a 17-year-old driving after drinking one and a half to two pints of lager or beer is 40 times more likely to have an accident than someone of his age who has not been drinking. Sometimes emotions may be heightened by alcohol consumption; a person may become aggressive or cry more easily. In extreme cases the person may go unconscious.

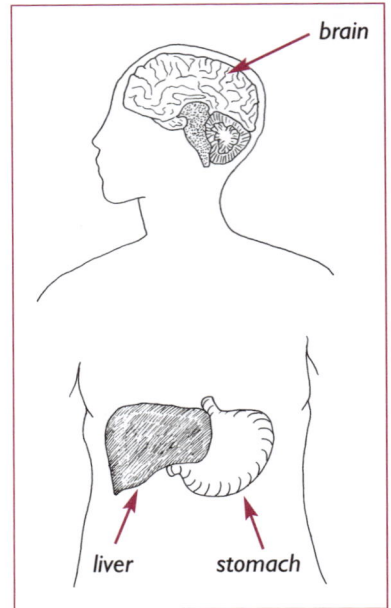

Effects of parental alcohol misuse

Given that approximately 1 in 10 Irish people are problem drinkers or alcohol misusers, there must be large numbers of Irish families affected by the problem. Children who grow up in a family where there is a problem drinker have a lot to cope with. The problem drinker can be very inconsistent: one minute the loving parent, the next a selfish drinker who doesn't seem to care how much hurt he or she causes. Sometimes the problem drinker can get violent or verbally abusive when drunk. This makes living with the person very stressful.

Studies of homes affected by alcohol misuse show that children in these families frequently take on one of four different personalities or roles in an effort to cope with living in a stressful environment. The four roles or personalities are as follows:

- Hero
- Scapegoat
- Lost child
- Mascot

Hero

This child works hard, is very mature and responsible. He or she tries to hold the family together and solve the family's problems. The hero wants to show the outside world that their family is a good, respectable one.

Scapegoat

This child appears to be the opposite of the hero. He or she gets into trouble in school and acts irresponsibly. When this child becomes a teenager, she or he is likely to break other rules, e.g. under-age drinking, drug use, sex from an early age. There is a high instance of unexpected teenage pregnancy among these children. The reason for the scapegoat's behaviour is to take attention away from the drinking parent. Everyone will be giving out and worried about the scapegoat, not the drinker.

Lost child

This child is quiet and very undemanding. He or she asks for nothing. This child sees all the trouble the drinker and the scapegoat are causing and thinks that if she or he is practically invisible that this will help the family's problems go away.

Mascot

The mascot is usually the youngest child in the family. He or she is treated like a baby by the rest of the family and told that there is nothing wrong. This child becomes very confused as a result.

When these children become adults, they do not suddenly drop these roles. Without help:

- The hero stays much as he or she is, and frequently marries someone who has a drink problem whom they can look after.

- The scapegoat is vulnerable to addiction.

- The lost child finds it hard to form close relationships.

- The mascot tries to remain a child and has trouble being responsible.

Listen to Jackie giving an account of her family on Track 6. Can you identify who is in each role?

Who is the hero? _____

Who is the scapegoat? _____

Who is the lost child? _____

Who is the mascot? _____

Alcohol and the law

Activity

Read the information and answer the questions that follow.

Because alcohol can be a dangerous drug, its use has always been controlled by society. Licensing laws state when, where and to whom alcohol can be sold. Other legal controls on the use of alcohol relate to drunkenness, drink driving and age restrictions on the sale of alcoholic drinks to young people.

Licencing laws

- Pubs, restaurants, hotels, sports and social clubs, if they are to allow people to buy and drink alcohol on the premises, must have a drinks licence. Drinks licences are granted by the courts.
- Off-licences have a licence to sell alcohol, but people cannot drink it on the premises.
- Pubs are allowed to open between 10.30 a.m. and 11.30 p.m. (12 p.m. summer) Monday-Wednesday. Thursday-Saturday opening times are 10.30 a.m.-12.30 a.m. unless the pub has an 'extension'. On a Sunday pubs may open all day from 12.30 p.m.-11.00 p.m.. (11.30 p.m. summer) Pubs must also close on Christmas Day and on Good Friday. Half an hour's drink-up time is allowed every day.
- It is permissible to brew beer and wine at home but not spirits such as poteen.

Age restrictions

- It is an offence to give alcohol to a child under five years of age, and children under 15 years are only allowed into a pub during permitted hours if they are accompanied by a parent or guardian.

- It is an offence to sell alcohol to a person under 18 years of age in either a pub or an off-licence. The pub or off-licence owner can be fined for doing so and their drinks licence endorsed.
- If you are under 18 it is against the law for you to buy or consume alcohol in a public place. If you do so, you may face a fine.
- If a garda suspects with 'reasonable cause' that you are under 18 and have bought or are consuming alcohol in a public place, you are obliged to give your correct name, age and address. If you give false details, you may face a fine. The garda can also confiscate the alcohol.
- You cannot work as a bar person if you are under the age of 18.

Drinking and driving

It is an offence to drive under the influence of alcohol. If you have more than 80 mg of alcohol per 100 ml of blood, you are deemed to be under the influence. This limit can be exceeded by some people if they drink only one pint of beer.

1. What age do you have to be to work in a pub? _____

2. What is the law in relation to home brewing?

_____

3. At what time can pubs open in the morning? _____

4. What is the legal winter closing time on a Tuesday?

_____

5. What is the legal summer closing time on a Saturday?

_____

6. What age must you be to buy alcohol? _____

7. What is the law in relation to drinking and driving?

_____

_____

8. When can a garda take alcohol from a young person?

_____

_____

9. Do you think there is a need for laws relating to alcohol?

Yes ☐   No ☐

Give a reason for your answer.

_____

_____

Activity

Investigate how smoking, alcohol and other drugs are portrayed in magazines and other print media. Present a collage of your findings.

Activity

Ask other groups in your school/centre to fill out this or a similar questionnaire. Present your results using bar charts, etc. Be sure to point out that there are no names on the questionnaires and that answers will be treated in confidence.

Alcohol questionnaire

Are you: Male ☐   Female ☐

Age group: 12-15 ☐
                            16-18 ☐
                     19 and over ☐

1. Do you drink alcohol?   Yes ☐   No ☐

2. If yes, how often? (Please tick)
   Once a week   ☐
   More than once a week   ☐
   Less than once a week   ☐

3. On average how much would you drink on a night out?
   1-4 drinks or units   ☐
   5-8 drinks or units   ☐
   More than 8 drinks or units   ☐

Note: I drink = $^1/2$ pint of beer, lager or cider, I shot of spirits or I glass of wine.

4. Have you ever been drunk?   Yes ☐   No ☐

5. Have you ever been sick as a result of drinking?
                                                 Yes ☐   No ☐

6. Have you ever forgotten parts of the night?
                                                 Yes ☐   No ☐

7. Attitudes to alcohol (Please tick)   Agree   Disagree

• Almost everybody drinks.   ☐   ☐

• You don't need to drink to have a good night.   ☐   ☐

• People who don't drink are generally 'dry'.   ☐   ☐

• Very few people develop problems with drink.   ☐   ☐

• Alcohol is responsible for many family problems. ☐   ☐

Key Assignment

For this key assignment you must collect information on healthy lifestyles. One of the best places to get this is on the internet. If you do not have access to the internet you could write to or telephone your local health promotion unit. Which one you write to depends on where in the country you are located. Pick the nearest one to you from the list below. (This activity will fulfil the second part of Key Assignment 2.)

When you have completed this key assignment, go to the beginning of this module and tick it off on the checklist.

Area covered	Address and Phone Number
Dublin (north)	Northern Area Health Board, Health Promotion Department, Unit 7, Swords Business Campus, Balheary Road., Swords, Co. Dublin. Tel. (01) 8823303.
Dublin (south)	South Western Area Health Board, Health Promotion Unit, 52 Broomhill Road., Tallaght, Dublin 24. Tel. (01) 4632800.
North-East	North Eastern Health Promotion Unit, Railway Street, Navan, Co. Meath. Tel. (046) 9076400.
Midlands	Midlands Health Promotion Unit, 3rd floor, The Mall, William Street, Tullamore, Co. Offaly. Tel. (0506) 46730.
Mid-West	Mid Western Health Promotion Unit, Parkview House, Pery Street, Limerick. Tel. (061) 316655.
North-West	North Western Health Promotion Unit, Main Street, Ballyshannon, Co. Donegal. Tel. (071) 9852000.
South-East	South Eastern Health Promotion Unit, Dean Street, Kilkenny. Tel. (056) 7761400.
South	Southern Health Promotion Unit, Eye, Ear and Throat Hospital, Western Road, Cork. Tel. (021) 4921641.
West	Health Promotion Services, Western Health Board, West City Centre, Seamus Kirk Road, Galway. Tel. (091) 548321.

Key Assignment

For this key assignment you must present a report on a drug that you studied as part of your Social Education course.

When you have completed this key assignment go to the beginning of this module and tick it off on the checklist.

Name of drug

_____

Write down five things you learned about the drug.

1. _____
2. _____
3. _____
4. _____
5. _____

List the effects of taking this drug:

Short-term effects

1. _____
2. _____
3. _____

Long-term effects

1. _____
2. _____
3. _____

In your opinion, what is the biggest risk someone takes by deciding to use this drug?

_____

Exam Time

Social Education (2002) – Short questions

1. A person must be 17 years of age to work as a bar person.
                                        True ☐   False ☐

2. Nicotine causes both physical and psychological dependence.
                                        True ☐   False ☐

3. The substances in this picture are examples of:

                    Stimulants ☐   Sedatives ☐

4. Fish, meat and poultry are all important sources of:
                    Calcium ☐   Protein ☐   Fibre ☐

Social Education (2003) – Short questions

5. A baby born to a mother who smokes is generally smaller.

    True ☐   False ☐

6. Excessive alcohol consumption on a regular basis can lead to epilepsy.

    True ☐   False ☐

7. In order to have a healthy balanced diet how many servings from the meat, fish and alternatives group should a person eat each day?

    6 ☐   4 ☐   2 ☐

8. A conviction for the use of cannabis can hinder you ability to travel abroad.

    True ☐   False ☐

9. What is the recommended maximum intake of alcohol for a fully-grown man per week?

    28 ☐   21 ☐   14 ☐

Social Education (2003) – Long question

10. Look carefully at the 'food box'.

FOOD BOX		
Yogurt	Fish	Cream
Oranges		Chips
Sugar	Bread	Salt	Biscuits
Pasta	Potatoes	Butter	Beef

From the 'food box' give one example each of the food that contains:

1. Carbohydrates   e.g.

_____

2. Vitamin C   e.g. _____

3. Iron   e.g. _____

11. Describe two ways in which HIV can be passed from person to person;

1. _____

2. _____

12. Look carefully at the picture below of a beautiful girl called Lorna Spinks and the picture of her about to die in hospital.

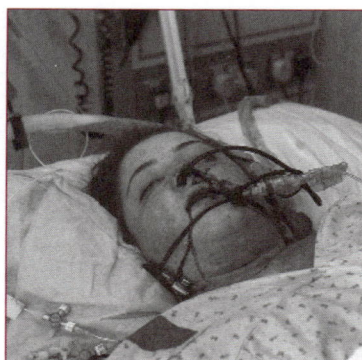

Lorna did not die because of a car accident. She didn't have a fall. This is Lorna after taking two 'E' pills. Her mother and father said that they hoped that this picture would serve as a warning to others. Her heartbroken mother said that her beautiful daughter died 'looking like a monster'. Police said she had taken two lime-coloured pills marked with a euro symbol before visiting a nightclub in Cambridge, where she was studying sociology. A family's life has been devastated and a very promising life destroyed. Lorna is the latest in a growing number of young people to die after taking Ecstasy.

A. Do you think that these pictures would stop young people from taking Ecstasy?

Yes ☐   No ☐

Explain _____

_____

B. When you take Ecstasy, you can't know what you're taking.

Agree ☐   Disagree ☐

Explain: _____

_____

C. Answer true or false to each of the following statements.
Ecstasy causes dehydration.   True ☐   False ☐
Ecstasy causes a rise in heartbeat and temperature.
                                                True ☐   False ☐
Ecstasy can cause users to experience flashbacks.
                                                True ☐   False ☐
Ecstasy can result in severe depression.   True ☐   False ☐

Social Education (2003) – Long question (part)

13. Despite health warnings and new laws people continue to smoke. Explain **one** reason why you think young people choose to smoke.

_____

_____

14. Approximately 90% of lung cancer victims smoke. Explain one other possible danger for people who smoke.

_____

_____

15. A. The five main categories of drugs are sedatives, hallucinogens, depressants, opiates and stimulants. Select two categories and give an example of each.

Category	Example

B. In the case of each example given, describe one effect and one risk involved in taking it.

Example: _____

Effect: _____

_____

Risk: _____

_____

Example: _____

Effect: _____

_____

Risk: _____

_____

C. 'Drug users hurt only themselves.' Explain whether you agree or disagree with this statement.

_____

_____

_____

Unit 3 *Relationships and Sexuality*

Sex Role or Gender Stereotyping

Sex role or gender stereotyping is when we have a fixed and over-simplified idea of what it means to be male or female. People who stereotype others according to their gender often have incorrect ideas about men and women's abilities, behaviour and life expectations.

Activity

Here are some examples of gender stereotyping. Can you think of two more?

• Girls just want to find a husband for themselves, settle down and have kids.

• Boys are no good at looking after young babies.

Now your turn:

Girls: _____

Boys: _____

Personality traits
Here is a list of personality traits. Put an 'F' beside the ones that are usually seen as female, and an 'M' beside those usually seen as male. Some may be both 'F' and 'M'.

Caring ☐	Fun-loving ☐	Tough ☐
Intelligent ☐	Generous ☐	Kind ☐
Studious ☐	Quiet ☐	Witty ☐
Sensitive ☐	Confident ☐	Patient ☐
Bad-tempered ☐	Aggressive ☐	Chatty ☐
Ambitious ☐	Carefree ☐	Fit ☐
Strong ☐	Honest ☐	Emotional ☐

Discuss your answers.

Abilities and expectations

Some people have fixed ideas about what men and women are good or bad at doing and what each should expect out of life. Read the statements below. Tick whether you agree or disagree with them. Afterwards discuss your answers.

	Agree	Disagree
Women are better at looking after children.	☐	☐
Men are better at maths.	☐	☐
Women are better at writing and spelling.	☐	☐
Women with young children should not go out to work.	☐	☐
Men should not have to do much housework.	☐	☐
Women spend money on foolish things.	☐	☐
Men sometimes have to put their job before their family.	☐	☐
Women sometimes have to put their job before their family.	☐	☐
Men should make the big decisions in the home.	☐	☐
Men are afraid of intelligent women.	☐	☐
Intelligent men are usually wimps.	☐	☐
Women are very emotional.	☐	☐
Men can do any job.	☐	☐
Women can do any job.	☐	☐
Men are only after one thing.	☐	☐
It is wrong for a man to have sex with lots of different women.	☐	☐
It is wrong for a woman to have sex with lots of different men.	☐	☐
Women should wear sexy clothes.	☐	☐
Very few girls are interested in sport.	☐	☐
Men who stay at home to mind the children are lazy.	☐	☐
Men in jobs like hairdressing and nursing are usually gay.	☐	☐

	Agree	Disagree
A woman boss would not be taken seriously.	☐	☐
Married men should earn more than married women.	☐	☐
A woman who delays having children to advance her career is not normal.	☐	☐
There is no need for girls to do subjects like woodwork.	☐	☐
There is no need for boys to do home economics.	☐	☐

How are gender stereotypes transmitted?

Activity

Can you think of three ways that gender stereotypes are transmitted? One example has been done to help you.

Young girls are often dressed in clothes and shoes that do not allow them to play physical games like football, in sand or other messy play.

_____

_____

_____

_____

Women in the Workforce

A good indicator of how society currently views males and females roles is by looking at workforce trends.

Activity

Look at some statistics from the 2002 census. Work out the percentages for males and females in each occupation and write them in the table.

Occupation	Numbers of females in occupation	% females in occupation	Numbers of males in occupation	% males in occupation
Secretary	30,250	_____	418	_____
Bank/Building society managers	3,332	_____	4,486	_____
Barristers/Solicitors	3,325	_____	4,703	_____
Dentists	539	_____	967	_____
Nurses	40,433	_____	3,674	_____
Chefs	8,562	_____	9,264	_____
Teachers (secondary)	17,510	_____	10,193	_____
School principals	931	_____	558	_____
Firefighters	46	_____	1,585	_____
Gardaí (Sergeant and below)	1,507	_____	9,420	_____
Gardaí (above Sergeant)	16	_____	474	_____
Army (Sergeant and below)	297	_____	6,636	_____
Army (above Sergeant)	49	_____	867	_____

Discuss what you think these figures tell us about how men and women's roles are viewed in society. From the figures do you think that societies attitudes are changing?

Track 7

On Track 7 you will hear a group of students and their teacher having a discussion about sex-role and gender-stereotyping. The discussion is divided into two parts. Listen carefully and answer the questions that follow.

Part 1

1. What definition of gender stereotyping did the class come up with?

_____

_____

_____

_____

_____

2. List four examples from the discussion of how men and women's *personalities* are sometimes sex-role or gender-stereotyped by society.

Men	Women
A _____	A _____
B. _____	B _____
C. _____	C _____
D. _____	D _____

Part 2

3. What definition of gender-*role* stereotyping did the class come up with?

_____

_____

_____

4. List four examples from the discussion of how men and women's *roles* are sex-role or gender-stereotyped by society.

Men's roles	Women's roles
A _____	A _____
B. _____	B _____
C. _____	C _____
D. _____	D _____

5. List four suggestions that the class made as to how ideas about sex-role or gender-stereotyping are formed.

A _____

B. _____

C. _____

D. _____

Key Assignment

For this key assignment you need to form a small group of 3-4 people. As a group collect pictures and information from magazines and newspapers and use it to make a collage illustrating ways in which the media promote sex-role stereotyping. Advertisements will be particularly useful.

When you have completed this key assignment, go to the beginning of this module and tick it off on the checklist.

Relationships

Unlike some animals that are solitary, people are social beings. Getting on with others and forming relationships is important to all of us. Many of us worry about how we appear to others. We worry about not being liked or accepted. This can be particularly true for teenagers and young adults when they start to want to form sexual relationships.

The ability to form relationships, whether they be sexual or not, does not come naturally to everyone. It is not a skill that we are born with, but one that we develop and perfect over the years. This is why people who do not see or experience healthy relationships during their childhood can find it difficult to form stable, loving relationships later in life.

Activity

Different relationships fulfil different needs in us. Some of these needs are listed in the box below. Can you name two significant people in your life and write beside each one what needs they fulfil in you.

Love	**Understanding**	**Food**	**Shelter**
Sexual fulfilment	**Belonging**		**Fun**
Acceptance	**Admiration** **Appreciation**		**Support**
Praise	**Stability**		**Protection**
Someone to talk to	**Companionship**		

Significant person 1 is   _____

The needs they fulfil for me are _____

Significant person 2 is   _____

The needs they fulfil for me are _____

List three qualities you would look for in a friend:

1 _____

2. _____

3. _____

Healthy choices about sexual relationships

When you were a young child you had very little input into decisions made by your parent(s). Generally you went where the rest of the family was going, and did what the rest of the family was doing. As you move into young adulthood, however, you have much more control over decisions made about your life. You probably spend more time with your friends than you do with your parents and the rest of your family. As a teenager or young adult you are developing your own value system. You are developing your own ideas of what behaviours are acceptable and unacceptable. Your friends, the media, etc. may have influence over what you do, but in the end the final choice is your decision.

Many of the decisions that you make as a teenager can have serious consequences for your future. One example are the decisions that you make about sexual behaviour. Sometimes it is thought that decisions about sexual behaviour have more important or serious consequences for girls than for boys. What do you think?

There are different factors that interfere or distort your ability to make the best decisions about risky behaviours. The most common one is the use of alcohol and other drugs. When under the influence of these, people are more likely to take risks that they would not normally take.

Track 8

Listen to Track 8 and answer the questions below. Orla's parents have arrived home early from a weekend away. They have caught Orla, who is 17, in bed with her boyfriend Peter, who is 21. They have sent Peter home and are now talking to Orla in the kitchen.

1. How does Orla justify her decision to have sex with Peter?

_____

_____

2. Why does Orla's father think that it is a bad idea for someone to be sexually active at Orla's age?

_____

_____

3. Why does Orla's mother think that it is a bad idea for someone to be sexually active at Orla's age?

_____

_____

4. Do you think that what Orla is doing is a good idea? Give a reason for your answer.

Yes ☐   No ☐

Reason:

_____
_____
_____

dearSusan

My friend is acting like a slut!

Dear Susan,
I am really worried about one of my very best friends. She is really getting a name for herself. Every Saturday night we go out and she gets drunk and ends up going home with a different guy each time. Usually the guys are a good bit older than her and she nearly always ends up having sex with them. I don't think she always uses protection as the last time she told me she thought she could be pregnant. Thank God it turned out to be a false alarm. I hate to see her disrespect herself like this, but what can I do?

Emily, 18, Waterford

Dear Emily,
You are right to be worried about your friend. If she is not practising safe sex, she is not only putting herself at risk of unplanned pregnancy but of sexually transmitted diseases as well. Do you think you could talk to her about the risks she is taking and perhaps pick up an information leaflet on STDs from your local health promotion unit or clinic for her to read? Unfortunately your friend doesn't seem to think too highly of herself at present.

The price of unprotected sex!

Dear Susan
I am a nineteen-year-old guy with a problem. I met this girl, let's call her Clare, about a month ago at a disco. Both of us had quite a bit to drink and we ended up having unprotected sex.
    About a week ago, I noticed a number of small warts on my penis and am very worried about them. I feel really angry towards this girl. What should I do?

Worried, 19, Donegal

Dear Worried,
It sounds like you have what are called genital warts. This is a very common sexually transmitted disease. The virus that causes genital warts can lie dormant in the system for up to six months so you may be blaming 'Clare' in the wrong.
    You will have to go to your GP. He or she will be able to tell you for certain and prescribe something to remove them. Unfortunately the virus that causes genital warts remains in the system so they may come back.

What do you think of the replies given to the problems in the letters to Susan? Would you have advised anything different? Write your opinion in the space below.

Problem 1

_____

_____

_____

_____

Problem 2

_____

_____

_____

_____

Reproduction

The female reproductive system

Label the diagram below:

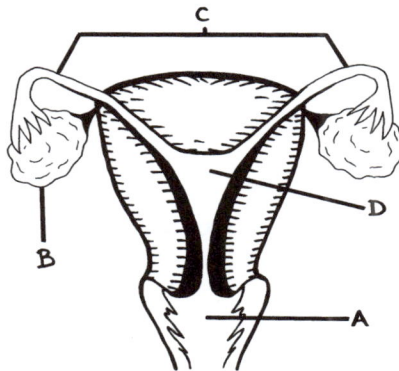

From puberty onwards a healthy female's ovaries release an egg or ovum once a month. This is called ovulation. The egg is released into one of two fallopian tubes which are located nearby. It stays in the fallopian tube for a few days waiting to be fertilised by male sperm.

If the egg is not fertilised, it continues on its way into the uterus or womb and out of the body. The woman then has her period as normal. If, on the other hand, the egg is fertilised this is called fertilisation or conception. The egg will make its way to the womb and implant or stick itself to the wall. The woman is now considered pregnant.

The female sex hormones progesterone and oestrogen are responsible for both ovulation and the development of secondary characteristics during puberty such as breast enlargement and the growth of pubic hair. These hormones are also responsible for the changes that occur to the female body during pregnancy.

The male reproductive system

Activity

Label the diagram below:

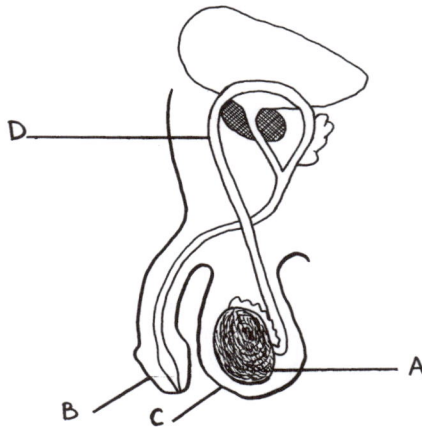

D
A
B   C

From puberty onwards, the male testes produce sperm. The testes are held outside the body in a sac called the scrotum. The testes also produce the male sex hormone testosterone, which is responsible for the production of sperm and causing changes at puberty such as the voice breaking, and the growth of pubic and facial hair.

When the male reaches orgasm during intercourse, sperm travels from the testes through tubes called the vas deferens to the penis where it is then released far up in the woman's vagina near the cervix. The sperm then swim frantically towards the woman's fallopian tubes in an effort to fertilise the egg, which may or may not be there. In the end only one sperm fertilises the egg, even though many thousands are released.

Pregnancy and Birth

Fertilisation takes place in the fallopian tubes.

After a few days the egg travels to the womb where it implants or sticks itself to the womb wall. The woman is now pregnant.

Sometimes the embryo does not remain implanted, and an early miscarriage follows. Some women do not even know they are pregnant and just think they are having a heavy period.

The placenta forms at the point where the embryo is implanted or stuck.

The embryo is now called a foetus.

The umbilical cord joins the placenta to the foetus.

Approximately 10% of babies are delivered by caesarean section. The woman's stomach and womb is cut open and the baby removed in this way. The most common reasons for this procedure are a very big baby, a small pelvis or when the baby is coming feet or buttocks first (breeched).

The placenta supplies the foetus with food and oxygen and takes away waste products.

The umbilical cord is cut and clamped and the baby is checked out.

Unfortunately some harmful substances such as alcohol, nicotine, heroin, cocaine, cannabis and some viruses such as HIV can pass to the baby as well.

After the head is delivered the rest of the baby usually comes out quite easily. The placenta and the rest of the afterbirth comes out then.

The head is usually delivered first. Sometimes a small cut is made in the vagina to make the opening bigger. A local anaesthetic is given before the cut is made. This is called an episiotomy and prevents tearing.

Contractions begin and a woman may request pain relief in the form of an epidural, which is given by injecting anaesthetic into the fluid surrounding the spine.

When the baby is ready to come, the waters sometimes break.

The baby usually remains in the womb for 40 weeks after the first day of the woman's last period. This is the due date.

Activity

Match these words and definitions.

1. A male sex hormone   __ a. Transition into adulthood
2. Vas deferens   __ b. Testosterone
3. Produce sperm   __ c. Fertilisation
4. Where the egg is fertilised __ d. Womb
5. Uterus   __ e. Releasing an egg every month
6. A female sex hormone   __ f. Fallopian tubes
7. Cervix   __ g. Joins testes to the penis
8. Puberty   __ h. Opening of the womb
9. Conception   __ i. Oestrogen
10. Ovulation   __ j. Testes

Answer the following questions on pregnancy in the spaces provided.

1. Name three functions of the placenta?

A. _____

B. _____

C. _____

2. Explain how women who drink, smoke or take other drugs while pregnant are putting their babies at risk.

_____

_____

3. What is an episiotomy?

_____

4. Give two reasons why a baby may be born by caesarean section.

A. _____

B. _____

Work out the due date:

Mary has just done a pregnancy test which has turned out positive. She now wants to calculate her expected due date. The first day of her last period was 6th October. When will the baby be due?

_____

Contraception

Information leaflets on contraception are available from the health promotion unit closest to you. Addresses and phone numbers were listed earlier in the chapter.

The Pill

There are two types: the combined Pill and progesterone only. The Pill makes the body think it is pregnant already and if taken every day at the same time it is very safe. It is available on prescription only.

Natural methods

By recording natural signs and symptoms, for example increases in temperature, couples can recognise the woman's fertile time. Couples avoid sex during this time. This is not a very reliable method and is usually used when religious beliefs do not permit the use of artificial methods.

Injectable contraceptives

An injection is given to the woman every 12 weeks, and works in the same way as the pill. It is a very safe method.

Coil

This is fitted into the womb by a doctor and stops the egg from implanting. It is a very safe method and is usually used after a woman has children.

Condoms

There are both male and female condoms. Both stop sperm entering the vagina. They must be used very carefully to be effective.

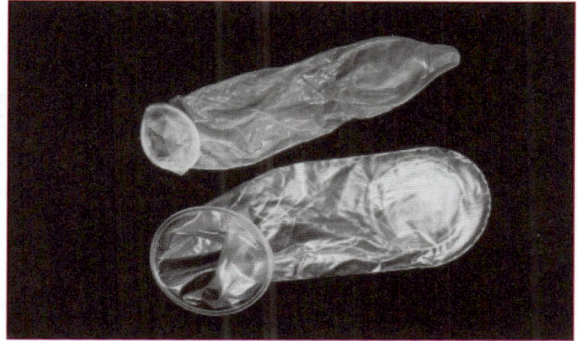

Male and female condoms

Diaphragm, also known as a cap

This is inserted into the vagina before intercourse and blocks sperm from travelling up to the egg. It must be used with a spermicide cream (which kills sperm).

Note: using a male condom is the only method that helps prevent the spread of sexually transmitted diseases.

HIV and AIDS

AIDS has been described as the plague of the twentieth century. The disease AIDS is the final, life-threatening illness caused by the HIV virus. The first cases of AIDS were identified in America in 1981, although researchers have evidence to show that the virus has been around in Central Africa from as early as the 1950s. At the end of 2003, it was estimated that there were 37 million adults and 2.5 million children worldwide infected with the virus (World Health Organisation 2004). When the HIV virus enters the body the person is said to be HIV positive. When the virus destroys large numbers of T-cells, which are a type of white blood cell, the person is said to have developed AIDS. White blood cells are used by us to fight disease. Without them we are prone to all sorts of illnesses and infections. It is one of these diseases, most commonly pneumonia, that eventually kills the AIDS victim. It may take as long as 15 years for someone who is HIV positive to develop AIDS.

There are three main ways that the HIV virus can spread. These are as follows:

- unprotected sexual intercourse with an infected person;
- intravenous drug users sharing needles with infected people;
- infected mother to her unborn child. There have been at least 65 babies born in Ireland with HIV (National Disease Surveillance Centre 2003);
- in the past, through transfusions (all blood is tested now).

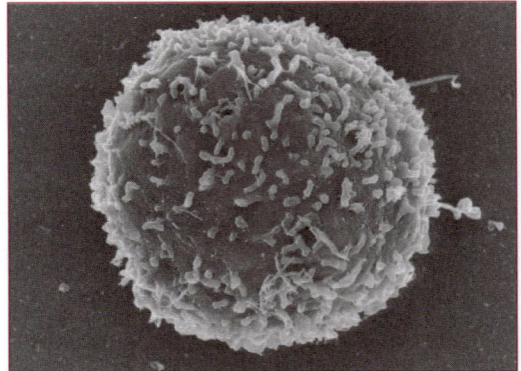

Normal T-cells

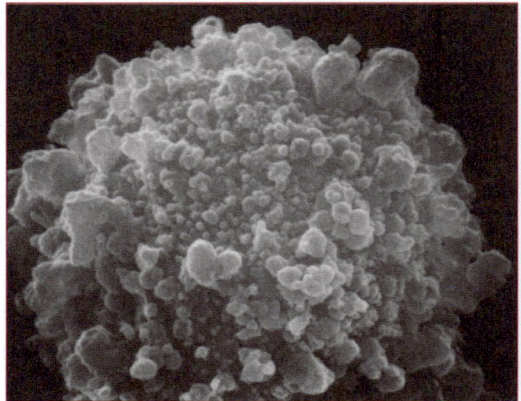

HIV-infected T-cells

Symptoms

Stage 1

No symptoms. During the first stages of HIV infection the symptoms do not show up. People can live with being HIV positive without even knowing it.

Stage 2

Mild illness. At this stage the virus grows within the white blood cells and destroys them. The white blood cells fight disease in our bodies and so when large numbers of them are destroyed, the body's defences weaken. The person may begin to feel frequently tired, lose weight or develop a cough, diarrhoea or fever and not be able to fight it.

Stage 3

Severe illness. By this time the virus has practically destroyed the body's immune system, so that it is not able to fight even the most common illnesses. Eventually the person picks up an illness that kills them. Pneumonia is a common one.

Treatment

Scientists have been trying very hard to find a cure for AIDS. As yet they have not been entirely successful. Efforts have been concentrated in three main areas:

- A drug or medicine which kills the virus once it enters the body.
- A vaccine that would make us immune to the disease.
- Education programmes about the dangers of AIDS, how it is spread and how it can be prevented.

In 1986 a drug called AZT was developed. AZT does not cure the disease, but it does prolong the life of the AIDS sufferer by trying to stop the virus reproducing. The trouble with developing a medicine that kills the HIV virus is that the virus actually gets inside the cells of the person's body. It is difficult to find a medicine that will kill the virus inside the cells and yet not kill the cell itself. AZT has side effects such as severe anaemia, which requires blood transfusions.

Activity

Answer the questions below.

1. How is AIDS different from HIV?

2. Explain the four main ways that HIV is or has been transmitted.

3. Benny has been sharing needles with his friends to inject steroids. Explain why Benny's sexual partner, Michelle, may be at risk of getting the HIV infection?

4. Many teenagers report that they do not use condoms when having sex. What are some of the reasons they might give for not using them?

5. Explain why an HIV-infected person is much more likely to get a chest infection than a non-infected person.

_____

_____

6. What is the main drug used in the treatment of AIDS patients?

_____

Living with AIDS: Terry's story

I vividly recall a night in December or January about a year ago. It was 6.00pm, very cold and getting dark. I was waiting for a bus to go home, standing behind a tree for protection from the wind.

I had recently lost a friend to AIDS. From whatever measure of intuition God had given me, I knew suddenly and quite certainly that I also had AIDS. I stood behind the tree and cried. I was afraid. I was alone and I thought I had lost everything that was ever dear to me. In that place, it was very easy to imagine losing my home, my family, my friends, and my job. The possibility of dying under that tree, in the cold, utterly cut off from any human love seemed very real. I prayed through my tears. Over and over, I prayed, 'Let this cup pass'. But I knew. Several months later, in April, the doctor told me what I had discovered for myself.

Now, it is nearly a year. I am still here, still working, still living, still learning how to love. There are some inconveniences. This morning, just out of curiosity, I counted the number of pills I have to take during the course of a week. It came to 112 assorted tablets and capsules. I go to the doctor once a month and find myself reassuring him that I feel quite well. He mutters to himself and re-reads the latest laboratory results which show my immune system declining to zero.

My last T-cell count was 10. A normal count is in the range of 800-1,600. I have been fighting painful sores in my mouth that make eating difficult. But, frankly, food has always been more important to me than a little pain. I have had thrush for a year. It never quite goes away. Recently, the doctor discovered the herpes virus had gotten hold of my system. There have been strange fungal infections. One was on my tongue. A biopsy caused my tongue to swell and I couldn't talk for a week, making many of my good friends secretly thankful. A way had been found to shut me up and they all revelled in the relative peace and quite. Of course, there are night sweats, fevers, swollen lymph glands, and unbelievable fatigue.

The head of the local health department in my area was quoted recently saying she believes there is a conspiracy of silence on AIDS. She reports that of the 187 deaths in this area from AIDS not one has listed AIDS as the cause of death in an obituary It appears that this conspiracy of silence involves those who have AIDS, or are infected with the virus, as well as the general public which still seems to have a difficult time discussing the subject.

Activity

1. When Terry was standing under the tree waiting for the bus he prayed for God to 'let this cup pass'. What do you think he meant by this?

2. What are T-cells and why is it serious for Terry to have such a low count?

3. What main health problems is Terry having?

4. Apart from Terry's health problems, what other problems do you think he may encounter in his everyday life?

5. Why do you think that out of the 187 deaths from AIDS in the area of the United States where Terry lives, no one wanted to declare AIDS publicly as the cause of death?

6. Imagine that you are Terry's partner. How do you think you would you feel and what do you think you would you do when Terry was first diagnosed as having AIDS?

Other Sexually Transmitted Diseases (STDs)

Sexually transmitted diseases are caused by various bacteria, viruses and fungi. They are passed from an infected person to a non-infected person through sexual activity. Sexually transmitted diseases can be prevented by avoiding high-risk behaviours. High risk behaviours include having multiple or many different sex partners, having sex without the man wearing a condom or having sex with people you don't know very well. A person may show no symptoms, yet still be infected and contagious.

STDs caused by bacteria

Syphillis

Approximately 50 cases present for treatment every year in Ireland.

Symptoms

The symptoms of syphillis occur in three stages:

Stage 1   Pimple like sores appear and disappear again.
Stage 2   Rash appears especially on hands and feet and there may be a temperature and headaches. These symptoms will also go away.
Stage 3   The disease attacks the brain and other organs; blindness, deafness, brain damage and heart attacks can then occur.

Treatment

Antibiotics, especially penicillium.

Gonorrhoea

Approximately 300 cases present for treatment every year in Ireland.

Symptoms

1-14 days after infection both men and women usually experience a burning sensation when urinating. There is then first a watery and then a thick, yellowish discharge from the penis or vagina. If the condition is not treated the bacteria may go to the fallopian tubes of women and cause a disease called pelvic inflamatory disease (PID). This disease can cause sterility or even death.

Babies born to mothers with the condition can develop eye problems, which can lead to blindness. In hospitals, drops are put into all babies eyes after birth to prevent this happening.

Treatment

Antibiotics.

Chlamydia

Approximately 1,400 cases present for treatment every year in Ireland.

Symptoms

Same as Gonorrhoea.

Treatment

Antibiotics.

STDs caused by fungi

The most common STD caused by a fungus is called candidiasis, or thrush. In men there are usually no symptoms, while in women there will be vaginal itching and a thick creamy white discharge. Thrush is treated with antibiotic creams or a vaginal pessary (a capsule of cream), which is placed high up in the vagina using an applicator.

STDs caused by parasites

Parasites are tiny creatures that live off humans and animals. Pubic lice and scabies are the most common examples. Both will cause itching in the pubic area and the scabies will also cause a rash. Medication will get rid of them.

STDs other than AIDS caused by viruses

Genital herpes

Approximately 270 cases present for treatment every year in Ireland.

Symptoms

Not all of the following symptoms may appear. There may be blister-like sores on and around the genitals, fever, and swollen glands. Women may have a discharge and men may feel pain when urinating. There is a risk of brain damage and even death to babies of infected women. Usually these babies are delivered by caesarean section, so they do not make contact with the vagina.

Treatment

There is no cure. Symptoms are treated with a drug called acyclovir.

Genital warts

Approximately 3,750 cases present for treatment every year in Ireland.

Symptoms

These look like the warts that appear on the hands. The warts can be removed but the virus that causes them remains in the body forever. This means that the warts can come back from time to time. Warts may not appear for six months after the person has been infected.

Treatment

There is no real cure, but the warts can be removed by a doctor or by using a cream.

Hepatitis B

There were 15 cases in 2000.

Symptoms

Hepatitis B attacks and damages the liver. Symptoms may not appear for six months after being infected. Symptoms include headaches, loss of appetite, fever, tiredness, nausea and vomiting. The person may appear yellow and jaundiced.

In the past, quite a few people got the disease because they were given transfusions of infected blood.

Treatment

There is no real cure but there is now a drug called alpha interferon which is sometimes given to treat symptoms.

Activity

1. How can you reduce the risk of contracting an STD?

_____

_____

2. Explain the statement, 'When you have sex with someone, you are having sex with everyone that person has had sex with.'

_____

_____

3. Which STDs should pregnant women have themselves tested for and why?

_____

_____

_____

Exam Time

Social Education (2002) – Short questions

1. Condoms reduce the risk of HIV infection.

    True ☐   False ☐

2. A woman who is pregnant must take which of the following to prevent spina bifida?

    Folic Acid ☐   Vitamins ☐   Starch ☐

Social Education (2003) – Short questions

3. A pregnant mother with AIDS cannot pass HIV on to her unborn child.

    True ☐   False ☐

Social Education (2004) – Short questions

4. Some sexually-transmitted infections can lead to infertility.

    True ☐   False ☐

5. The unequal treatment of people based on gender is:

    Ageism ☐   Sexism ☐   Racism ☐

Module 2

My Community

This module should be completed during session 1 (Year 1).

Below are seven key assignments for this module. You should choose FOUR of these. One of them must be a group activity and one must be an out-of-school activity. As you work through the module and complete the assignments you have chosen, come back to this page and tick off each of them.

1. I contributed several images/newspaper cuttings to a class collage about our local area.
   Date: _____

2. I took part in a class discussion about our local area in the past. I made at least three contributions to this discussion.
   Date: _____

3. I interviewed a senior citizen from my local community about life in the past.
   Date: _____

4. I designed and presented a simple leaflet about five different organisations providing a service for young people in my area.
   Date: _____

5. I plotted a long distance journey by road on a map from my home to another point more than one hundred kilometres away. On this map I marked in the major towns, the distances to them and between them. I also showed an alternative route to this point using a different mode of transport.
   Date: _____

6. I went to my local library and got the names of at least five useful resources/books on the history of my area.
   Date: _____

7. I plotted on a map the litter bins provided by the local authority/authorities on my route to school.
   Date: _____

Unit 1 *Research Skills*

One of the features of the Leaving Certificate Applied programme is that it encourages you to find out things for yourself. To be able to do this you need to have research skills. In this unit you will be looking at a number of different research methods. Throughout the two years you will be able to use these methods in all your subjects. The methods that will be looked at in this chapter are:

- Surveys
- Questionnaires
- Interviews

Other sources of information are your school or local library and of course the internet.

You will also be looking at how the information you gather can be presented by creating charts and tables.

Surveys

Surveys are used when you do not want very detailed information. Because surveys are generally conducted on the spot they cannot be very long or complicated. Surveys give the researcher a general picture.

Stages in conducting a survey

You must think about what it is you want to find out about or test. This is called your hypothesis. Examples of hypotheses are, 'most students in our school/centre get here by bus', or 'most people in this school come from families of three children or less'.

The next thing you have to do is to select your sample. Say you are investigating the hypothesis – 'that more teenage girls smoke than teenage boys'. It would not be possible to survey all teenage boys and girls, so you must therefore select a sample. You must be careful that your sample is representative of the group you are trying to find out about, which in this case is teenage boys and girls. Your sample cannot be too small or narrow. If you surveyed five girls and one boy about smoking, this would not be representative of teenagers. The sample is too small and not enough boys were questioned.

If time does not allow you to survey a big sample, you can restrict your hypothesis. For example you may say, 'I wish to investigate whether smoking is more common among Leaving Certificate Applied girls than boys in my school/centre'.

When you have decided on your hypothesis and your sample, you must then decide on a small number of clear questions.

You need then to think of a way of recording your results. A good idea is to get a clipboard and clip-on sheets like the one shown. This allows you to record a number of results on the one sheet of paper.

You then count up your results and afterwards present your findings. You can present your findings using bar charts, pie charts or tables. This makes them easy to read and look more interesting.

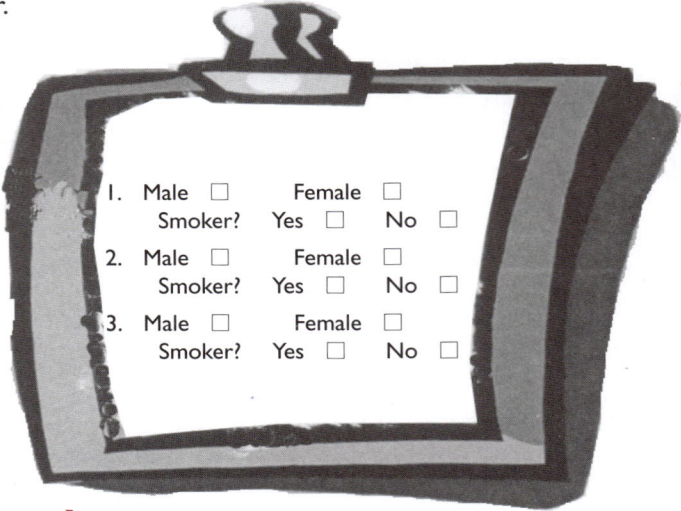

1. Male ☐   Female ☐
        Smoker?   Yes ☐   No ☐
2. Male ☐   Female ☐
        Smoker?   Yes ☐   No ☐
3. Male ☐   Female ☐
        Smoker?   Yes ☐   No ☐

Presentation of results

Percentage of smokers classified by gender

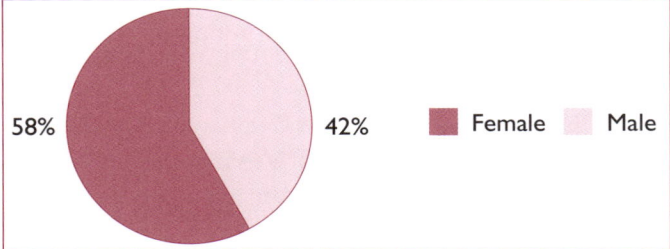

58%   42%   ■ Female   ■ Male

58% of teenage smokers are girls

Activity

Carry out a survey and present your results to the rest of the class. Perhaps your computer teacher could show you how to create pie charts like the one above to present your data.

Questionnaires

Questionnaires give us more detail than surveys and are a very common way of getting information about people's behaviour and beliefs. A questionnaire only works if the people who are filling it out understand what they are being asked and want to answer the questions being asked. This is why a questionnaire must be really well designed. If a questionnaire is badly designed people will either not fill it out at all or will be confused.

Designing a good questionnaire: points to remember

1. Only use one side of the paper.

2. Give the questionnaire a heading to show what it is about.

3. Give a paragraph of introduction at the beginning of the questionnaire.

4. Give clear instructions in bold capitals, e.g. TICK THE ANSWER WHICH MOST APPLIES TO YOU.

5. Keep the questionnaire as short as possible. Space out the questions well and leave room for answers.

6. Avoid too many open-ended questions, for example:

   What do you like most about the Leaving Certificate Applied? _____

   If you include a lot of open-ended questions like this one where you could get a hundred different answers, recording and presenting your findings will be very hard.

7. If the matter you are investigating is of a sensitive nature, put the most straightforward non-threatening questions first. Leave the more sensitive ones to last. For example, if you were asking people to fill out a questionnaire on alcohol misuse you would not open with the question:

   Do you think you drink too much?   Yes ☐   No ☐

8. Confidentiality is very important. People who fill out your questionnaire need to know that you will not be telling everyone what they have written. It is a good idea to put at the top of the questionnaire:

   Do not write your name on this questionnaire. I would like to assure you that your answers will be treated with the strictest confidence.

9. It is usually advisable to carry out what is called a pilot study. A pilot study is when you give a draft copy of your questionnaire to a small number of people. When they fill it out, they give you feedback. They may be able to point out to you questions they found confusing or other things they felt could be improved upon. You can then design the final questionnaire taking into account the comments you received in the pilot study.

10. At the end of the questionnaire you should write:
Thank you for your help.

Activity

Fill out the questionnaire below on the Leaving Certificate Applied.

LEAVING CERTIFICATE APPLIED QUESTIONNAIRE

Dear fellow student,

I am carrying out an investigation into levels of satisfaction among LCA students with the LCA course. I would appreciate it if you would fill out the questions below as honestly as you can. Do not write your name on the questionnaire. I would like to assure you that your answers will be treated in strictest confidence.

Yours sincerely,

Maura Duffy

Maura Duffy

1. How many people are in your group? (PLEASE TICK)

0-10 ☐   11-18 ☐   19-25 ☐   26 or more ☐

2. Is your group mixed? (both male and female)

   (PLEASE TICK)   Yes ☐   No ☐

3. What two specialisms are you taking as part of your LCA programme?

   A. _____

   B. _____

4. Has anyone else in your immediate family (mother, father, brother or sister) completed a leaving certificate?

   (PLEASE TICK)   Yes ☐   No ☐

5. Are your parents pleased that you have chosen to stay on to do your Leaving Certificate? (PLEASE TICK THE ANSWER THAT MOST APPLIES TO YOU)

Very pleased   Quite pleased   Don't really care   Not pleased
☐   ☐   ☐   ☐

6. Overall, how satisfied are you with the Leaving Certificate Applied programme?

(GIVE YOUR ANSWER A RATING BETWEEN 1-10)
(10 IS EXTREMELY SATISFIED, WHILE 1 IS EXTREMELY DISSATISFIED) _____

7. What do you like about the LCA programme?

(WRITE 1 BESIDE THE BEST THING, 2 BESIDE THE NEXT BEST AND SO ON)

A. You get marks throughout the two years which means not everything goes on the exams at the end. ☐

B. I find the new subjects very interesting. ☐

C. I like the way the subjects are relevant to our lives. ☐

D. Things like work experience prepare us for real life after school. ☐

E. Doing tasks and key assignments gives me a great sense of achievement. ☐

F. We get little, if any, homework. ☐

Other (please specify) _____ ☐

8. What do you dislike about the LCA programme? (Please tick)

A. Tasks are too much work ☐

B. It is not as good as the traditional leaving certificate. ☐

C. There isn't much choice of subjects ☐

D. Other (please specify) _____ ☐

What is your favourite LCA subject? _____
Why?
_____
_____

Thank you for taking the time to fill out this questionnaire.

Interviewing

Interviewing is another popular method of getting information from people. The main advantage of interviewing is that unlike surveys and questionnaires you can get very detailed information. The main disadvantage is that interviewing is very time-consuming and so you can only have a small sample. This could effect the accuracy of the results.

Preparing to interview someone

1. Think about what information you need and then set out the questions you wish to ask in a logical way.

2. You could do a practice or a pilot interview with a member of your own group.

3. It is usually best to tape the interview so that you are not interrupting the conversation trying to take notes.

4. Contact the person and, if they agree to be interviewed, set a time and a place to conduct the interview.

5. Start the interview by telling the person what your project is about and why you are interviewing them.

6. Begin the interview with easy, non-threatening questions; leave the sensitive ones, if there are any, until last.

7. At the end of the interview thank the person for their time.

8. Listen to your tape as soon as possible after the interview. Write out what was said. This is called transcription. Transcriptions are frequently put in the appendix of a piece of research.

Track 9

On Track 9 you will hear an interview. Lorna, the interviewer, is interested in music and would like to be a DJ when she leaves school. She is interviewing a DJ from a local radio station about his job. His name is Joseph Ryan. Listen to the interview 3-4 times and make a rough transcription of what is said. You will have to stop and start Track 9 to do this.

Presenting Research Results: Creating Charts

When you have completed your research and come up with a set of results you must now present it in a way that is both attractive, interesting to look at and easy to understand. Below are some of the ways that information can be presented:

Smoking among 13-18 year olds

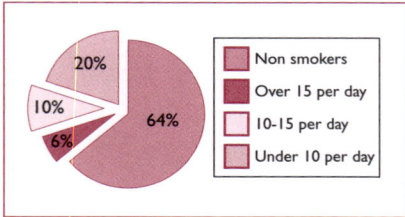

- Non smokers
- Over 15 per day
- 10-15 per day
- Under 10 per day

20%
10%
6%
64%

Pie chart

% of students doing Leaving Cert.

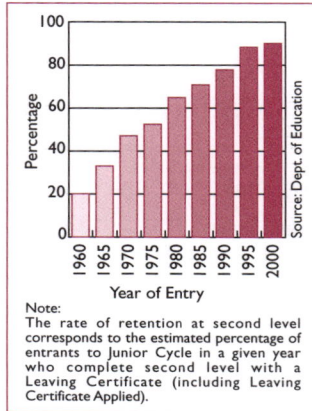

Percentage
Year of Entry
Source: Dept. of Education

Note:
The rate of retention at second level corresponds to the estimated percentage of entrants to Junior Cycle in a given year who complete second level with a Leaving Certificate (including Leaving Certificate Applied).

Bar charts

Students at second level

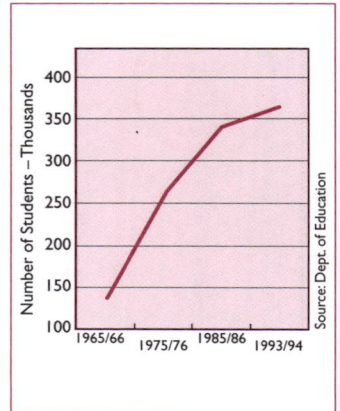

Number of Students – Thousands
Source: Dept. of Education

1965/66   1975/76   1985/86   1993/94

Line graph

Tables

	Engineering	Technical Drawing	Construction Studies	Maths (higher only)	Physics	Chemistry
Boys	98%	97%	98%	64%	78%	64%
Girls	2%	3%	2%	36%	22%	36%

Proportion of boys/girls completing a selection of Leaving Certificate subjects (1990)

Activity

Look at the charts above and answer the questions.

1. Approximately what percentage of pupils entering secondary school in 1980 went on to do their Leaving Certificate? _____

2. What percentage of teenagers smoke more than 15 cigarettes a day? _____

3. Approximately how many students were there at second level during the academic year 1965/66? _____

4. In 1990 what percentage of those sitting Leaving Certificate physics were girls? _____

Exam Time

Social Education (2003) – short question

1. This graph is an example of which type of chart?

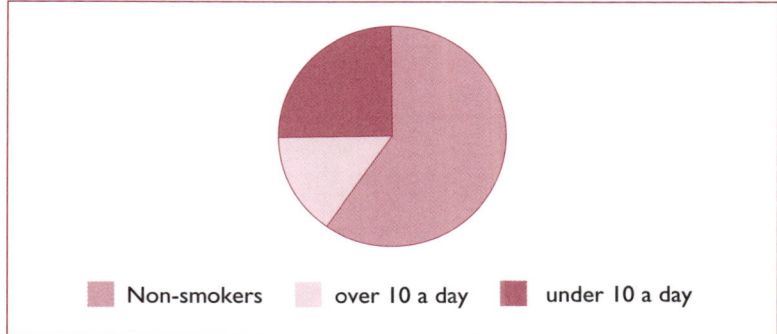

Non-smokers   over 10 a day   under 10 a day

Bar Graph ☐   Pie chart ☐   Line chart ☐

Social Education (2004) – short question

2. According to the information given which of the following statements is correct?

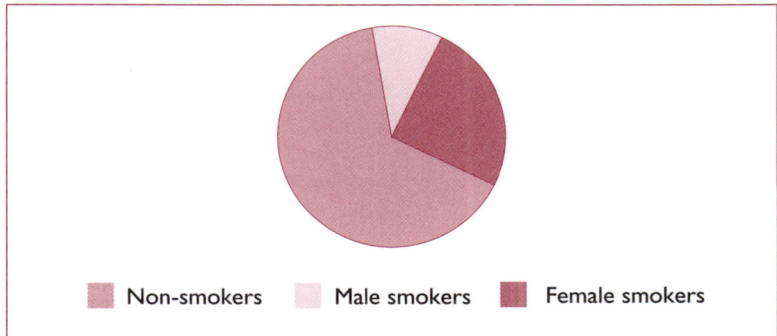

Non-smokers   Male smokers   Female smokers

The majority of the staff smokes.   ☐

More women than men smoke.   ☐

Smokers account for approximately 25 per cent of the staff.   ☐

Unit 2 *My Own Place*

It is well known that for humans to be content within themselves they need a sense of place. You only have to consider the number of people of Irish descent that come here searching for their roots every year to see that knowing where you come from is very important to people.

Activity

On the map on the next page:

1. Circle the town you live in or the nearest town to you in red pen.

2. Draw a line showing your county boundary.

3. Name the counties touching the county in which you live.

   _____

4. Mark in blue and name the river nearest to where you live.

5. Colour in the mountain range that is nearest to where you live.

6. In blue pen, circle on the map three towns close to where you live.

7. Name a lake close to your school/centre.

   _____

8. Can your town or area be easily accessed by each of the following?

Sea	Yes ☐	No ☐
Air	Yes ☐	No ☐
Rail	Yes ☐	No ☐

The map for the activity above gives a general idea of where you live and what geographical features there are in your area. If you want to look more closely at an area you need a much more detailed map. These maps are called Ordnance Survey maps because they are produced by the Ordnance Survey Office in the Phoenix Park in Dublin. Ordnance Survey maps can be very detailed. The map you will be working on next has a scale of 1000:1, this means that every millimetre on the map represents one metre in reality.

rivers
over 160m
over 300m

DONEGAL
TYRONE
DERRY
ANTRIM
DOWN
FERMANAGH
LEITRIM
SLIGO
ARMAGH
MONAGHAN
LOUTH
CAVAN
MAYO
ROSCOMMON
LONGFORD
MEATH
WESTMEATH
GALWAY
DUBLIN
OFFALY
KILDARE
LAOIS
WICKLOW
CLARE
CARLOW
TIPPERARY
KILKENNY
LIMERICK
WEXFORD
KERRY
WATERFORD
CORK

Letterkenny, Derry, Limavady, Coleraine, Ballymoney, Larne, Ballymena, Ballintra, Lifford, Strabane, Magherafelt, Newtownabbey, Bangor, Belfast, Hollywood, Comber, Donegal, Omagh, Dungannon, Lurgan, Portadown, Armagh, Banbridge, Downpatrick, Ballyshannon, Enniskillen, Newry, Manorhamilton, Monaghan, Clones, Keady, Sligo, Newtownbutler, Ballybay, Castleblayney, Belmullet, Inniscrone, Ballyconnell, Cootehill, Carrickmacross, Dundalk, Ballina, Drumshanbo, Cavan, Shercock, Tobercurry, Carrick-on-Shannon, Baileborough, Ardee, Knock, Boyle, Castlebar, Kells, Drogheda, Claremorris, Strokestown, Granard, Castlerea, Longford, Edgeworthstown, Navan, Balbriggan, Ballymahon, Castlepollard, Tuam, Roscommon, Mullingar, Delvin, Trim, Dunshaughlin, Athlone, Ashbourne, Swords, Ballinasloe, Ferbane, Tullamore, Edenderry, Leixlip, Dublin, Galway, Loughrea, Birr, Mountmellick, Kildare, Naas, Newbridge, Tallaght, Ballybrack, Bray, Portarlington, Monasterevan, Roundwood, Lahinch, Ennis, Mountmellick, Portlaoise, Athy, Rathdangan, Wicklow, Abbeyleix, Castledermot, Tullow, Arklow, Nenagh, Templemore, Castlecomer, Carlow, Gorey, Kilkee, Kilrush, Shannon, Thurles, Kilkenny, Muine Bheag, Ferns, Limerick, Gowran, Enniscorthy, Adare, Tipperary, Newcastle West, Clonmel, New Ross, Wexford, Listowel, Carrick-on-Suir, Tralee, Waterford, Tramore, Dingle, Mallow, Dungarvan, Killarney, Cork, Cobh, Bandon, Skibbereen

Activity

On the map on the next page, find out the answers to the following questions.

1. Imagine you live at 2 Beechwood Drive. What type of house do you live in? _____

2. Name two other house types shown on the map.
   (1) _____ (2) _____

3. Imagine you live at 7 Marian Road. What house numbers are either side of you? _____

4. What is between 18 Marian Road and the children's playground? _____

5. What is opposite 16 Main Street? _____

6. Number 3 Chapel Street is a chip shop. If there is a fire in the chip shop where would the fire brigade hook up their equipment? _____

7. You live at 15 Beechwood Drive and have no phone. Using the scale ruler at the bottom of the map and a piece of paper, calculate how far you would have to travel to:
   (1) the nearest public phone box. _____
   (2) post a letter. _____

8. Name 3 recreational facilities on the map.

   _____

   _____

   _____

9. What type of area is represented on the map? (Tick one)
   (1) A large town ☐   (3) A new urban development ☐
   (2) A section of a city ☐ (4) A small rural town ☐
   Give a reason for your choice.

   _____

10. Think of one advantage to living in an area like this.

   _____

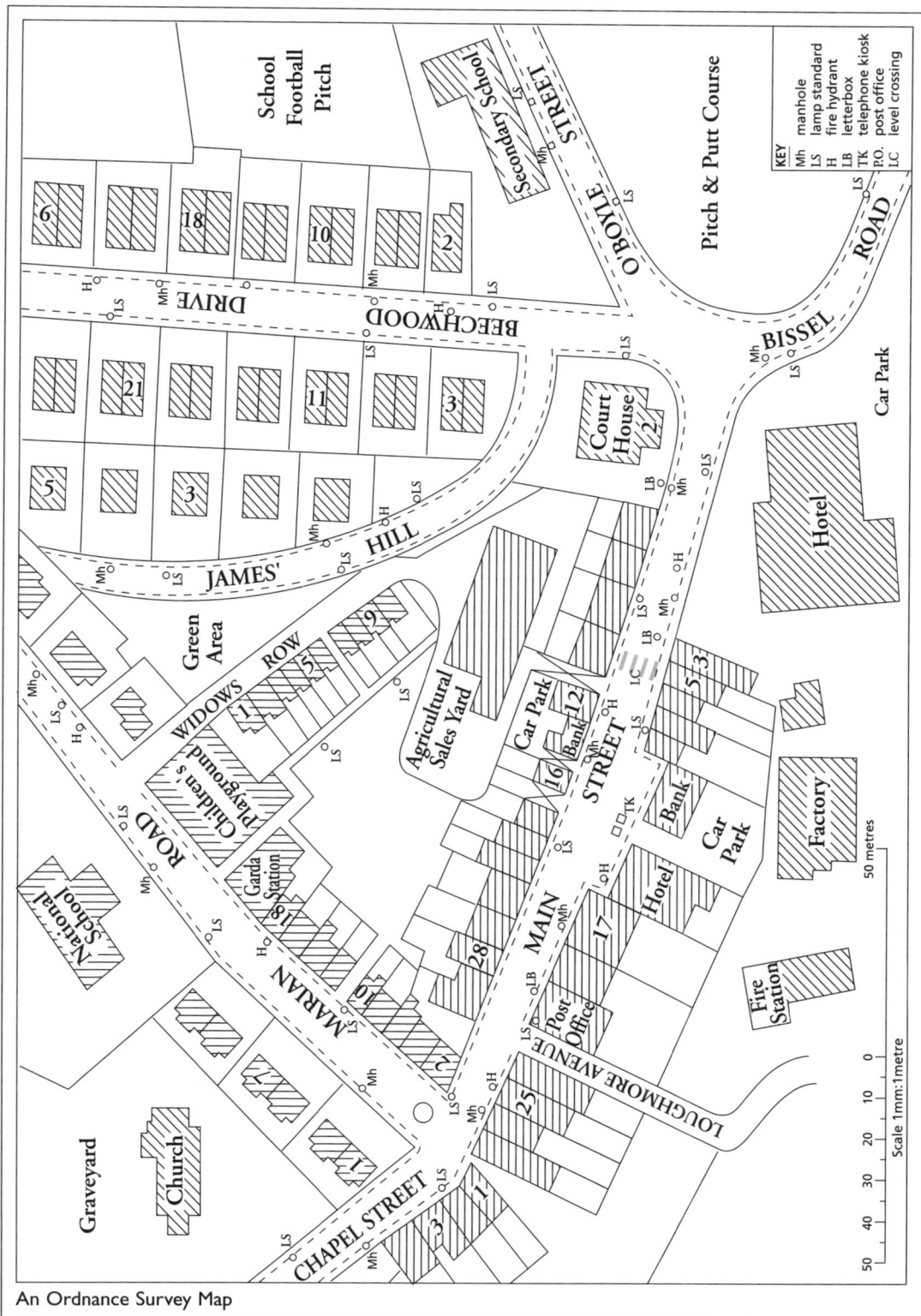

An Ordnance Survey Map

Activity

1. Find an Ordnance Survey map that covers the area where your school/centre is and identify features such as your school/centre, your home, roads, churches, shopping centres, wooded areas, etc.

2. Below is a section of an Irish road map. Imagine you are travelling by car from Naas to Gorey. List the villages and towns you would pass through.

_____

_____

_____

Note the scale at the bottom of the map. Approximately how far is the journey in kilometres? _____

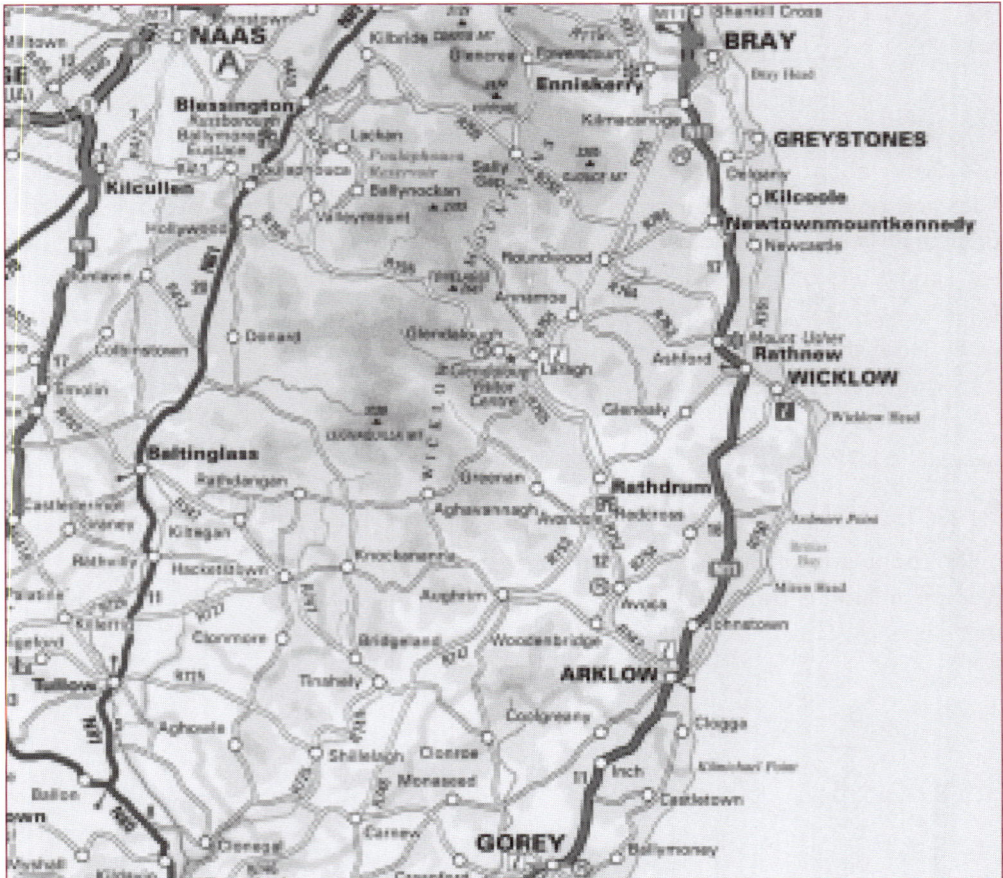

| 1:633,600 10 miles to 1 inch | 0 5 10 20 30 40 miles |
| | 0 5 10 20 30 40 50 60 kilometres |

Key Assignment

For this key assignment you must plot a long-distance journey by road on a map from your home to another point more than one hundred kilometres away. (Some tourist offices supply free road maps.) On this map, mark in the major towns and the distances to and between them. You must also explain how you could make the journey using a different mode of transport.

Use the route planner facility on the website at www.aaroadwatch.ie to plot this or another journey.

When you have completed this key assignment, go to the beginning of this module and tick it off on the checklist.

The Census

Usually every five years a census is conducted in this country. On the night of the census every household must fill in the census form, giving details of everyone staying in that house that night. The purpose of a census is to get accurate information about the people of our country. This information is then used for the planning of government services and policies. All information written on the census form is treated in strictest confidence. It is compulsory to participate in the census and failure to do so can result in a fine. The results of the census are usually made available to the public about one year after the census was conducted. They can be studied in the county library, but cannot be removed from there. Census results can also be downloaded from the Central Statistics Office website at www.cso.ie.

The census tries to get an accurate picture of trends such as:

Overall population

The 2002 population figure of over 3.9 million is the highest since 1871.

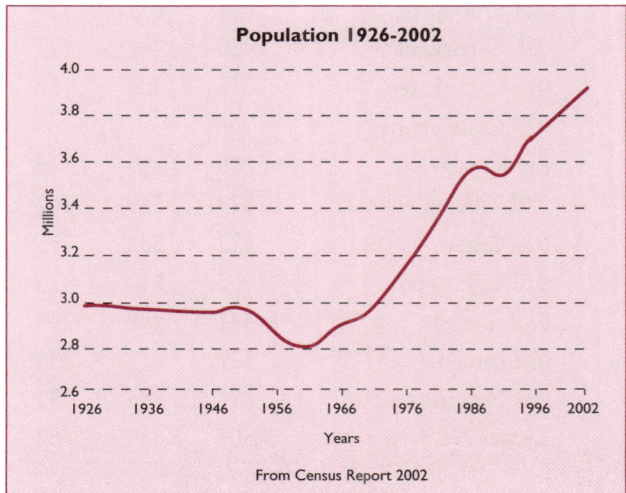

Population 1926-2002

From Census Report 2002

Population of different areas

- Geographic distribution (what areas are heavily populated and what areas are not)
- Age and sex composition of population
- Marital status
- Living arrangements, e.g. numbers of lone parents, cohabiting couples, old people living alone, etc.

The census, as you can imagine, contains a huge amount of data, so is usually contained in several volumes or books.

Activity

Below is an example of the information that was gathered by the 2002 census. Study the information and answer the questions that follow.

Population and area of each Province, County, County Borough, Urban District, Rural District and District Electoral Divison/Ward, 1996 and 2002

District	1996	2002	2002		Change in Population 1996-2002		Area (hectares)
	Persons	Persons	Males	Females	Actual	Percentage	
Monaghan county (contd.)							
Castleblayney rural area	8,990	9,351	4,808	4,543	361	4.0	26,064
020 Annyalla	517	546	291	255	29	5.6	1,908
021 Ballybay Rural	1,210	1,181	575	606	-29	-2.4	1,889
022 Ballybay Urban	474	437	213	224	-37	-7.8	24
023 Bellatrain	225	211	117	94	-14	-6.2	1,073
024 Broomfield	600	652	328	324	52	8.7	2,004
025 Carrickaslane	450	462	232	230	12	2.7	2,036
026 Carrickatee	375	304	168	136	-41	-11.9	1,486
027 Castleblayney Rural (part)	1,889	2,228	1,118	1,110	339	17.9	2,676
028 Church Hill	529	569	302	267	40	7.6	2,461
029 Creeve	522	538	295	243	16	3.1	2,498
030 Cremartin	907	910	475	435	3	0.3	2,623
031 Greagh	432	448	244	204	16	3.7	1,616
032 Laragh	539	512	258	254	-27	-5.0	1,552
034 Mullyash	351	353	192	161	2	0.6	2,208
Clones No. 1 rural area	5,304	5,435	2,782	2,653	131	2.5	25,946

District	1996 Persons	2002 Persons	2002 Males	Females	Change in Population 1996-2002 Actual	Percentage	Area (hectares)
035 Aghabog	314	303	162	141	-11	-3.5	2,176
036 Anny	338	359	186	173	21	6.2	2,186
036 Clones Rural (part)	869	868	432	436	-1	-0.1	2,734
037 Cormeen	447	457	238	219	10	2.2	2,357
038 Currin	557	530	271	259	-27	-4.8	2,488
039 Dawsongrove	566	643	320	323	77	13.6	2,508
040 Drum	193	182	98	84	-11	-5.7	1,626
041 Drummully	98	102	56	46	4	4.1	981
042 Killeevan	348	357	192	165	9	2.6	1,734
043 Killynenagh	170	174	79	95	4	2.4	1,704
044 Lisnaveane	362	385	211	174	23	6.4	2,205
045 Newbliss	673	666	335	331	-7	-1.0	1,893
046 St. Tierney	369	409	202	207	40	10.8	1,354

1. Has the population of Newbliss increased or decreased between1996 and 2002? (please tick)
Increased ☐   Decreased ☐   By how much? _____

2. How many males were in Ballybay (urban and rural) the night the 2002 census was taken? _____

Activity

Go to your local library or look up the Central Statistics Office website at www.cso.ie and find out the following information about the population of your county and area.

Note: Volume 1 Population Classified by Area will give this information.

1. What is the present (last census) population of your county?

_____

2. What is the present (last census) population of your area, i.e. town, village.

_____

3. Has the population of your area increased or decreased between the last two census?

Increased ☐   Decreased ☐   By how much? _____

4. Can you give a possible reason for the increase/decrease in population?

_____

_____

_____

Exam Time

Social Education (2003) – Short questions

1. A census gives information about:

   Population ☐   Energy supply ☐   Politics ☐

Unit 3 *My Family in the Local Area*

Family History and Family Trees

About a family: Patricia's story

My great-grandfather on my mother's side was born in 1885. His name was Peter Sheridan. He came to this area of County Monaghan from an industrial school for orphans to find work in about 1900. He hadn't much formal education but was by all accounts a very intelligent man. He started work as a farm hand for a local landowner, and it is here that he learned his trade. He became what is called a quack. A quack was a sort of vet, who cured animals using herbs and other homemade medicines. Quacks were very well respected people around this area in the past. In addition to being a quack, my great-grandfather was also a drover. This meant that he spent some of his time transporting cattle on foot from one area of the country to another. His way of life meant that he was never long in the one place. This is probably part of the reason why he did not get married until he was over 40 years old. He married my great-grandmother, who was at the time only 19 years of age. Her name was Mary Brady. She, too, was not from the area but came here to find work as a maid in another of the big houses in the area. When she got married, the large farmer she was working for gave her a cow and a half dozen hens as a wedding present. They built a small cottage, and lived there until they died many years later.

Mary Brady had two children, the oldest of whom was my grandmother Kathleen Sheridan. The youngest child, James, died at about 6 months of what was thought to be measles.

When my grandmother finished primary school, she worked for a while in the big house, and when she was old enough, went over to England to train as a nurse. She returned in the 1940s and got married to my grandfather, Bernard Flannigan, whose parents' names (my other great-grandparents) were Mick Flannigan and Bridie Mathews. My mother, Ellen Flannigan, was my grandparents' youngest child. She had three brothers – Brian, Aidan and Paul.

My great-grandfather on my father's side came from Dundalk, a town about 30 miles away. His name was Paddy Walsh and he was a sailor.

He worked on the cargo ships that travelled between Liverpool and Dundalk. He married my great-grandmother, Alice O' Brien, in 1926. Like many other sailors of the time he refused to learn to swim and in fact drowned in rough seas some years later. Before this tragic event they lived in a small terraced house in the middle of the town and had five children. The oldest of these children was my grandfather, Eamonn Walsh. When he grew up, he got a job in the post office in the town and married my grandmother, Elizabeth O'Shea. My grandmother's parents were called Peter O'Shea and Elizabeth Murphy. My father, Eoin Walsh, was their oldest child.

Both sets of grandparents worked very hard and did the best they could for my parents. Neither family was rich, but nevertheless both my mother and father went to secondary school. This was the first time this level of education was achieved in my family and it was quite unusual in that according to my father only about 6,000 people sat the Leaving Certificate the year he did. After doing the Leaving Certificate, both my mother and father went to work in the bank, and this is where they met. They got married and well here I am! I am 17 years old and doing my Leaving Certificate. I hope to go to college in Dublin when I finish school to study architecture. I found researching my family story a little confusing at times, but all the same I enjoyed doing it.

Activity

Answer the questions about Patricia's family.

1. Name two jobs done by Patricia's relatives that are rare in Ireland today.
A. _____   B. _____

2. What is a drover? _____

3. What did James Sheridan die of? _____
Would this be likely to happen today? Give a reason for your answer.

Yes ☐   No ☐

Reason: _____

4. Try to find out and write down some of the jobs held by your relatives in the past.

_____
_____

5. Think of one way that Patricia's life is very different from that of her grandparents and great-grandparents.

_____

6. Would you like to have lived back in your great-grandparents' time? Give a reason for your answer.

Yes ☐   No ☐

Reason: _____

_____

Activity

Use Patricia's family story as a guide to help you to do yours. You might like to include pictures of your relatives to brighten it up.

Activity

1. Fill in Patricia's family tree.

Patricia's Family Tree

Maternal (mother's) side

Great-grandfather Great-grandmother
(Grandmother's parents)

Great-grandfather Great-grandmother
(Grandfather's parents)

Grandfather   Grandmother

Mother

Paternal (father's) side

Great-grandfather Great-grandmother
(grandmother's parents)

Great-grandfather Great-grandmother
(grandfather's parents)

Grandfather   Grandmother

Father

Note: this is a very simple family tree as only parents are represented on it.
You might like to include brothers and sisters on yours.

2. Research and present your own family tree.

Track 10

Roisin has decided to interview her grandmother about her life. Listen to Track 10 and answer the questions that follow.

1. Write down two changes that have occured in education since Roisin's grandmother was at school?

A. _____

B. _____

2. Roisin's granny said that her brother Paddy died of TB. Find out what this is.

_____

_____

3. Do you think that religion had a bigger part to play in people's lives in the past compared with today? Give a reason for your answer.

_____

_____

4. 'Women's lives have changed more drastically than men's over the past 60 years.' Would you agree with this statement? Give a reason for your answer.

_____

_____

5. What three world events did Roisin's granny most remember?

A. _____

B. _____

C. _____

6. In years to come what world events will you most remember?

_____

_____

Key Assignment

Use Roisin's interview with her granny as a guide to interviewing a senior member of your own family about life in the past in your community. This exercise can be used to fulfil the requirements of the third key assignment listed for this module.

When you have completed this key assignment, go to the beginning of this module and tick it off on the checklist.

Unit 4 *My Own Place in the Past*

Key Assignment

For this key assignment you need to go to your local library and get the names of at least five useful resources/books on the history of your area. Write the names of them below as evidence of having completed this key assignment.

When you have completed this key assignment, go to the beginning of this module and tick it off on the checklist.

1. _____
2. _____
3. _____
4. _____
5. _____

Key Assignment

For this key assignment your class group need to make a collage about your local area. Each member of the group must contribute something to the collage. Photographs, postcards, press cuttings or drawings of your own can be used. Present your class collage on a large sheet of paper. Keep it safe as evidence of having completed this key assignment. Your collage could compare how your area looks now to how it looked in the past.

When you have completed this key assignment, go to the beginning of this module and tick it off on the checklist.

Newgrange is the most visited tourist attraction in Ireland.

Activity

Research some historical sites in your area. Write about your findings in the space provided. Stick a picture or a photograph of your chosen site(s) into the space below.

An historical site in my area

Stick a photograph or drawing here

Key Assignment

For this key assignment you need to take part in a discussion about your local area in the past. You must try to make at least three contributions to this discussion.

When you have completed this key assignment, go to the beginning of this module and tick it off on the checklist.

Activity

Find out as much as you can about a famous person from your area. They could be a famous poet, politician, musician, sports person, writer, etc. They do not have to be from the past; they can be still living. Try to find a photograph to make your presentation more interesting.

Unit 5 *Community Amenities/Resources*

Areas with a strong community spirit usually have a host of clubs and organisations that are only too happy to have new members join. In this unit you are required to find out about the various clubs and organisations that are in your area. Use the work card below to guide you.

Activity

Think about the number of different clubs and organisations in your area. Look at the list and tick whether any exists in your area or not. Do not take too narrow a view of your area, it means within a few miles of where you live and not just on your doorstep.

Hobbies (sporting)

Snooker	Yes ☐	No ☐
Boxing	Yes ☐	No ☐
Golf	Yes ☐	No ☐
Pitch & putt	Yes ☐	No ☐
Gaelic football	Yes ☐	No ☐
Hurling	Yes ☐	No ☐
Camogie	Yes ☐	No ☐
Hockey	Yes ☐	No ☐
Gym	Yes ☐	No ☐
Basketball	Yes ☐	No ☐
Tennis	Yes ☐	No ☐
Fishing	Yes ☐	No ☐
Badminton	Yes ☐	No ☐
Swimming	Yes ☐	No ☐
Children's playground	Yes ☐	No ☐
Park or walkway	Yes ☐	No ☐

Hobbies (non-sporting)

Gardening	Yes ☐	No ☐
Bridge	Yes ☐	No ☐
Chess	Yes ☐	No ☐
Drama	Yes ☐	No ☐
Music	Yes ☐	No ☐

Charity Work

St. Vincent de Paul	Yes ☐	No ☐
Cerebral palsy	Yes ☐	No ☐
Barnardo's	Yes ☐	No ☐

Community Welfare

ISPCC	Yes ☐	No ☐
Homework club	Yes ☐	No ☐
Parent and toddler group	Yes ☐	No ☐

Can you think of other clubs or organisations in your area not mentioned in the list?

_____

_____

_____

Tourism in Your Local Area

Tourism is one of Ireland's biggest and fastest growing industries. Tourism currently employs over 133,000 people in this country and the number is rising every year. Certain areas of Ireland are well developed as tourist locations but others, while they have potential, are not so well developed.

Accommodation

Hotels	Yes ☐	No ☐
B&Bs	Yes ☐	No ☐
Campsites/caravan parks	Yes ☐	No ☐
Youth hostels	Yes ☐	No ☐

Transport

Good rail service	Yes ☐	No ☐
Good bus service	Yes ☐	No ☐
Is there much traffic congestion?	Yes ☐	No ☐

Other

Does your area hold any special events or festivals that would attract tourists?	Yes ☐	No ☐
Is your area relatively litter free?	Yes ☐	No ☐
Is your area relatively crime free?	Yes ☐	No ☐
Would you consider your area to be attractive for tourists?	Yes ☐	No ☐

Tourism symbols

Symbols

General Facilities

Symbol	Meaning
km	Distance from town
ⓒ	Price reduction for children
✖	Open all year except Christmas
⓺	Access for disabled persons
ⓟ	Car parking
▦	Central heating
⊞	Elevator/lift
⓰	Conference facilities
⌂	Within 2 km of sandy beach
✎	Baby-sitting service
⚲	Facilities for pets
⚲	Facilities for guide dogs
CC	Credit cards accepted
✻	Garden for visitors' use
⚶	Family friendly hotel (Facilities for children)
✠	Experience a working farm
G	Irish spoken

Bedroom Facilities

🛏	Total number of rooms
⍩	Number of rooms with bath/shower and toilet
🛏	Cot available

Symbol	Meaning
BX	No smoking bedrooms
🍽	Light meals available
☕	Tea and coffee facilities
✆	Direct dial from bedrooms
TV	TV in bedrooms

Meals and Drinks Facilities

ⓓ	Licensed to sell alcoholic drink
ⓨ	Licensed to sell wine only
alc	Á la carte meals only
�	Table d'hôte dinner

Sports Facilities

Symbol	Meaning
⛢	Bicycles for hire
✐	Angling facilities
∪	Horse riding/pony trekking facilities
✎	Games room
ⓖ	Gym only
⌂	Leisure complex
↷	Outdoor swimming pool
↶	Indoor swimming pool
✗	Squash court
⛁	Sauna only
⚲	Tennis court
●	Snooker (full size table)
⚑	Golf

Using the tourism symbols and your own local knowlege, prepare and present a tourist brochure for your area. Include information on each of the following:

- Tourism attractions
- Accommodation
- Eating options
- Shopping
- Transport
- Cultural activities
- Entertainment
- Special interest activities, e.g. hiking, horse riding, golf, fishing, canoeing, sailing, cruising, etc.

You will need to visit your nearest tourist office to get much of the information and photographs, etc. These will make your presentation more interesting. Again, your information technology teacher may advise you on how to improve the presentation of your brochure.

Industry in my local area

There are basically three different types of industries:

Primary industry   In years gone by this was a very common sort of industry. Primary industry basically means extracting the earth's natural resources and selling them, either directly to the public or to a secondary industry that will process them. Coal mining or growing crops is an example of a primary industry.

Secondary industry This type of industry processes the products of primary industry. For example, buying corn from a primary industry and making cornflakes out of it.

Service industry   This provides a service for the public rather than making goods. Tourism is largely a service industry.

List the main industries and sources of employment in your area. Place them under one of the three headings – Primary, secondary or service.

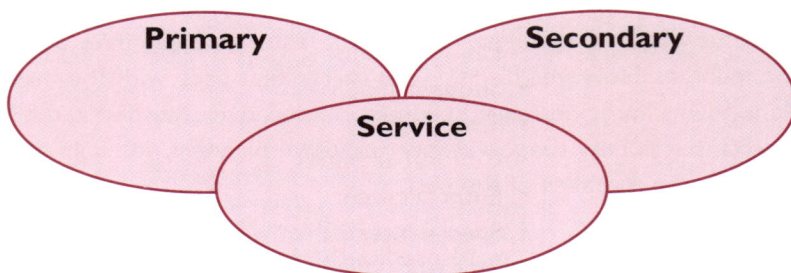

Primary

Secondary

Service

Pick three of the industries that you have mentioned above and write down why you think each of the three have decided to base their industry in your area.

Industry 1 _____
Reason for location in your area:

_____
_____

Industry 2 _____
Reason for location in your area:

_____
_____

Industry 3 _____
Reason for location in your area:

_____
_____

Find out what agencies promote industry in your area. Write two of them down:
1._____
2._____

Unit 6 *Planning in My Own Place*

City or Town Planning

Planning began with the first towns and cities in about 3500 BC. Our ancestors set aside areas for housing, worship and other activities. They built walls around their towns for protection against enemies. Throughout history, people have done some planning for their communities. However, planning has rarely kept pace with the huge growth in urban areas. Many towns and cities have become polluted, overcrowded and have huge traffic problems. It is now the job of city and town planners not only to plan for the future but to repair the mistakes of the past.

Town and city planners try to predict the future. They attempt to forecast such developments as large changes in population and industrial activity. Town and city planners work for the government. They develop run-down areas and plan recreational areas, such as parks and green belts, and new industrial areas. They also try to improve road network and parking facilities.

Most towns and cities in this country now have what is called a development plan. This plan is an overall vision for the community and is reviewed every five years. When it is being reviewed, members of the public can put in objections to it if they wish. Once completed, this plan can be examined in your local planning office during office hours. Closely related to this development plan is the concept of zoning.

Zoning

Zoning is a procedure that regulates the use of land. Town and city planners who work for the government divide up areas into different zones. Each zone has a different use, for example an area could be zoned as commercial, industrial, green belt or residential. Zoning means that towns and cities appear more attractive, function better and are healthier places to live. Zoning also means that when you buy property, you have a good idea what building will be permitted beside you. For example, if you buy a house in an area zoned as residential, you can be pretty sure that a huge factory will not be built next door. Having said this, land can be re-zoned by your local authority. This could mean, for example, a residential area being re-zoned as commercial and a shopping centre being built on it.

Activity

In this country, town and city planners work for the local authorities. Look in the green pages at the beginning of the telephone directory to find out the address and telephone number of your local authority. Write what you find below.

(Local authorities can either be county councils, borough corporations or county boroughs depending on where you live.)

_____

_____

Activity

Visit your local planning office and ask to view the development plan for your area.

Activity

How well-planned is your local town/area?

1. Are there good parking facilities in your town/area? ☐ ☐

2. Is there bad traffic congestion in your town/area during rush hour? ☐ ☐

3. Is there a public park in your town/area? ☐ ☐

4. Is there a children's playground in your town/area? ☐ ☐

5. Is there a good shopping centre in your town/area? ☐ ☐

6. Are schools situated near residential areas? ☐ ☐

7. Have large housing estates got services such as shops, etc., nearby? ☐ ☐

8. Are there facilities for travellers in your area? ☐ ☐

9. Have run-down parts of your town/area been redeveloped? ☐ ☐

10. Are historical buildings in your town/area in a good state of repair? ☐ ☐

11. Is there an industrial estate outside the town/area? ☐ ☐

12. Is there a public library in your town/area? ☐ ☐

13. Is there an arts centre or other cultural centre in your town/area? ☐ ☐

14. Is there a public swimming pool in your town/area? ☐ ☐

15. Is there a soccer or football pitch in your town/area? ☐ ☐

16. Is there a leisure complex in your town/area? ☐ ☐

17. Is your town/area bypassed? ☐ ☐

Planning Permission for Houses

When is planning permission needed?

Planning permission is needed if you want to build something, e.g. a house, or change the use of an existing building, e.g. make your house into a playschool. Planning permission is not needed for small house extensions as long as they are (a) to the back of the house, (b) under 23 metres square, and (c) not taller than the house. Planning permission is important because otherwise people could build what they want where they want and this would not be for the common good.

What types of permission are there?

- Full permission • Outline permission • Approval

To apply for planning permission you contact the planning authority for your area, i.e. county council, county borough, borough corporation or urban district council.

Full permission

This is the most common form applied for. To be granted this, you need to know exactly what house or extension you want to build. You must submit the following:

- Application form
- Detailed house plans
- Site plan – showing where house is located on the site
- Ordnance Survey map with site shown on it
- Site notice
- Advertisement from local paper
- Application fee.

Outline permission

People apply for this type of permission to see if the planning office will agree with their proposal in principle. Detailed plans are not submitted at this stage but at a later stage when approval is being sought.

Some people go ahead and build first and then apply for retention afterwards. This is not to be recommended as you can by law be asked to remove the building.

Getting planning permission from start to finish, if it is not objected to, usually takes three months.

If you want to know more about planning, the Department of the Environment have published a series of 11 information leaflets on the subject. These can be obtained from your local planning authority.

Exam Time

Social Education (2003) – Short questions
1. Planning permission is **not** needed if you want to:

Build a house ☐   Change windows ☐
Change the use of a building ☐

Social Education (2004) – Short questions
2. Applications for planning permission should be made to:

The Institute of Architects ☐   The local authority ☐
An Bord Pleanalá ☐

3. People applying for planning permission are required to place a notice in the newspaper.

True ☐   False ☐

Social Education (2003) – Long question
4. Read the letter and answer the questions that follow.

St. Paul's N.S

Dear Sir,

As chairperson of the board of management of St. Paul's National School I am writing to you to express our deep concern about the proposed landfill dump, which will be located just 500 metres from our school.

We believe that this dump will attract rats, which will bring disease. The increased volume of traffic on our roads will create more road traffic accidents. The constant foul smells and dangerous gases will pollute the air our children must breathe. There is also a potential threat to underground water and soil when chemicals seep underground. Added to all this is the massive damage this dump will do to the natural beauty of the area.

Because of all this we earnestly plead with you to stop the proposed location of this dump.

Yours sincerely,

J. Davis

Mr. J. Davies, Chairperson

A. This letter was written on behalf of what organisation?

_____

B. Name **three** potential dangers which the landfill dump could cause to the area.

_____

_____

_____

C. Local Authorities (County Councils and Corporations) are responsible for the environment in your area. Describe **two** other services which they provide.

_____

_____

D. Name **two** organisations that work for young people in your area and explain what they do.

_____

_____

4. In the past humankind was told:

> TREAT THE EARTH WELL; IT WAS NOT GIVEN TO YOU BY YOUR PARENTS IT WAS LOANED TO YOU BY YOUR CHILDREN.
>
> Old Indian Proverb

> EVERY PERSON HAS A DUTY TO PROTECT THE ENVIRONMENT.
>
> Draft Declaration on the Environment (1994)

List **three** ways that you can help to protect the environment in your area.

1. _____

2. _____

3. _____

Module 3

Contemporary Issues 1

This module should be completed during session 2 (Year 1).

Below are six key assignments for this module. You should choose FOUR of these; one must be a group activity and one an out-of-school activity. As you work through the module and complete your chosen assignments, come back to this page and tick off each of them.

1. I took part in a roleplay (as a participant or observer) and recorded my observations about a situation where the denial of a human right was at issue.
   Date: _____

2. I informed the class about a human rights issue/ campaign I found in the newspaper or elsewhere.
   Date: _____

3. I created an A1-sized promotional poster upholding one of the rights in the Universal Declaration of Human Rights.
   Date: _____

4. I explained to my class three things I considered right and three things I considered wrong with regard to a particular contemporary issue.
   Date: _____

5. I contacted an organisation/centre outside school that had information about a contemporary issue and gave a report to my class about what I had found out.
   Date: _____

6. With other members of my class I organised a survey on attitudes in our local area to a particular contemporary issue.
   Date: _____

Unit 1 *Social Context of Contemporary Issues*

The third module in social education is called Contemporary Issues 1. During your study of this module you will be investigating and finding out about issues that are important to you. You will be asked to report back on your findings as part of the four key assignments. Before you begin this module, it makes sense to first of all investigate what the term 'contemporary issues' actually means.

Activity

Discuss what you think 'contemporary issues' means and write your answers below.

Our class think the word 'contemporary' means:

_____

_____

The dictionary says the word 'contemporary' means:

_____

_____

Our class think the word 'issue' means:

_____

_____

The dictionary says the word 'issue' means:

_____

_____

Activity

Below is a list of contemporary issues. Go through the list, writing down whether each issue is of importance to you or not. Give a short reason for your answer. The first one has been done as an example.

Issues

Drugs in sport   Of interest ☐   Not of interest ✔

Reason *I never watch sport and don't play it, so I don't care what they do!*

Crime against the elderly Of interest ☐   Not of interest ☐

Reason _____

Issues

Homelessness	Of interest ☐	Not of interest ☐

Reason _____

Unemployment   Of interest ☐   Not of interest ☐

Reason _____

Alcohol abuse   Of interest ☐   Not of interest ☐

Reason _____

The troubles in the North Of interest ☐   Not of interest ☐

Reason _____

Vandalism   Of interest ☐   Not of interest ☐

Reason _____

Racism   Of interest ☐   Not of interest ☐

Reason _____

Third World poverty   Of interest ☐   Not of interest ☐

Reason _____

Child labour in India   Of interest ☐   Not of interest ☐

Reason _____

Here are some more issues for you to discuss:

AIDS   *Equality for the disabled*   Rape

Conflict   **Smoking**   Lone parents   Sectarianism

Divorce   *Child abuse*   Equality for women

Nuclear power   **Emigration**   *Poverty*

Joyriding   **Refugees**   *Recycling*   *Workplace bullying*

Pollution   *Traveller rights*   **Slave labour**

Ozone layer   Bullying   **Homelessness**

Irish Republican Army   Unemployment

Genocide   *Child labour*   **Crime**   *Death penalty*

Alcohol abuse   *Drugs*   **Early school leavers**

National and Global Issues

When you read an article about an issue in your local newspaper or listen to a discussion about an issue on local radio, you frequently see the issue only in terms of the problems that it causes locally.

Most issues, however, cause problems on a much wider scale. Issues grow to national and global importance.

Activity

Below is a list of local issues. Can you broaden them to national and global levels? The first one has been done as an example.

Issue	Local level	National level	Global level
Pollution	Opposition to new town dump	Pollution of Irish Sea by Sellafield	Hole in the ozone layer
Prejudice	Refugee is in hospital after racist attack		
Homelessness	Homeless man dies of exposure		
Drug abuse	Used needles found in kids' playground		
Conflict	Feuding families disturb peace with street brawl at two in the morning		

Note: For your contemporary issue task next year you will be required to look at the issue you choose to investigate from a local, national and global perspective.

Unit 2 *Forces/Interests*

Local Issues Explored

Read the articles taken from a number of provincial newspapers. When you have read the articles, answer the questions on them.

Cancer Rate Sparks Probe by Watchdog

Drogheda and its high incidence of cancer is to be examined in detail by the National Cancer Registry. Minister for Health Micheal Martin has confirmed that he has asked the cancer-monitoring body, which has statutory responsibility for the collation and analysis of data on incidence and prevalence of cancer in Ireland, to look more closely at Drogheda. Local TDs Fergus O'Dowd and Arthur Morgan have both been pushing for action following the publication of the report 'Cancer Mortality and Morbidity in Co. Louth', which revealed an alarmingly high number of cancer deaths in the Drogheda and Dundalk area, an area directly across the Irish Sea from the Sellafield nuclear power plant in Cumbria.

Deputy Morgan welcomed the commitment received from the minister that the cancer registry will investigate the findings of the recently published report, commissioned by Cooley Environment and Health Group (CEHG) from Dr. Dennis Pringle. The Sinn Fein TD also chairs the CEHG.

'The figures revealed in our study raise very alarming questions about the level of cancer in the Drogheda area and a specific investigation is urgently required. There are also other questions in relation to health issues in Drogheda, such as the high rates of asthma, especially in young children,' he said.

This report raises additional concerns about the proposed incinerator just three miles from Drogheda. 'It is more important than ever that the campaign to defeat this incinerator has a positive outcome, it should be a major issue in the local government election campaign.'

**Drogheda Independent
7 April 2004**

Activity

1. What two health problems have a higher than average incidence in the Drogheda area of County Louth?

2. What is the Minister for Health doing about the issue?

3. Name one group interested in this issue?

6. Many people believe that the Sellafield nuclear power plant in Cumbria is responsible for high levels of miscarriage, cancer and other health problems along the east coast of Ireland. Find out what you can about the Sellafield plant and the health implications it may have/has for Ireland.

'Run Dealers Out of Town' Says Grieving Mum

THE grief-stricken mother of a young Wexford man who died on Monday from an apparent heroin overdose says drug dealers should be run out of town.

"They are getting away with murder," said heartbroken Ann Whelan whose son Patrick, aged 27, was found dead by one of his brothers at a house on Trinity Street, on Monday afternoon.

His tragic death came just over a month since 24-year-old Martin Keane died from a suspected drugs overdose in an apartment less than a mile away.

Choking backs tears, Ann Whelan said her husband Gerry had told the gardaí who the drug dealers were and the time was long past to take off the kid gloves.

"If the dealers weren't there, our children wouldn't be able to go and get the drugs. Drug dealers are at every corner, they have to be taken off the streets," she said.

A Wexford councillor, speaking following the tragedy, said people caught dealing hard drugs on the streets of Wexford should be tried for manslaughter.

"Heroin is something new in Wexford and people don't know what they are taking. I believe they are overdosing by accident," said Cllr. Anna Fenlon.

"The word on the streets is that there's plenty of it (heroin) around and it worries me. If people are caught for dealing drugs, they should be charged with manslaughter. There needs to be a real deterrent and it's not there at the moment," said Cllr. Fenlon.

Expressing sympathy with the Whelan family, Sgt. Mick Walsh, at Wexford Garda Barracks, said it was a tragedy that another young man had apparently lost his life through drugs.

"The amount of heroin in the town is a problem, but I don't think Wexford is any worse than any other town of its size," said Sgt. Walsh.

He said the gardaí were aware of who was dealing drugs in Wexford, but the difficulty was in obtaining evidence that would stand up in court.

(Some names and place names have been changed to respect the privacy of the people involved.)

Wexford People
13 May 2004

1. This article places the blame for the drug issue at the door of the drug dealer – what do you think?

_____

_____

_____

2. Look through back issues of your local paper and try to locate articles dealing with the drugs issue in your area. A very useful website is www.unison.ie/allpapers.php3 that allows you to browse through a large variety of regional papers. You will have to register with them (it is free) to access their archives.

3. What services are available for people with drug problems in your area?

_____

_____

Donegal Town – 'Worse Than Ibiza Uncovered'

After a weekend which saw five separate assaults, road carnage that nearly resulted in a death and damage to the garda station, a long serving garda has said that Donegal town is becoming 'worse than Ibiza uncovered'.

The guard, who preferred not to be named, said it was a 'mystery and a miracle' that someone had not been killed in a public order incident in the town already. Blaming a widespread decline in moral standard and the lack of responsibility on the part of publicans and low manpower in the gardaí, the guard said the 'chain of causation' between what happens on a bar stool and what happens in the street afterwards needed to be recognised. "Publicans have a

duty of care. It should not be up to a handful of guards to babysit these people after someone else has allowed them to lose their mind on alcohol. In law there is a 'chain of causation' and I think the courts need to look at this and see if there is a direct correlation between what someone does after drinking, in relation to how much they have been allowed to drink."

On Friday night in Donegal town a youth was assaulted on Tir Chonaill Street in the town at about 4am. According to the guard there had been a row in a nightclub earlier which led to the alcohol-fuelled incident. "There were five fellas attacking one young lad. Luckily the boy's father happened along and

intervened, he stopped his son from getting a bad hiding." Inquiries are being made and a file is being prepared for the DPP. According to the guard, there were three separate and unrelated assaults on Tir Chonaill Street between Saturday night and Sunday morning. In one incident a youth had his nose broken. "To me the level of drinking going on among young people is now chronic," he said.

A potentially devastating incident in Ballintra on Sunday was also being investigated as being allegedly drink-related. At 3pm in the afternoon a youth in his 20s caused several hundred euros worth of damage when he drove a car down the main street of Ballintra at an estimated 80mph and collided with two cars, one of which had a man sitting in it. "It was nothing short of a miracle that this man was not killed. Both cars were severely damaged, it was a very serious impact and the two passenger sides of both cars were ruined," said the guards.

Later on Sunday night, at about 7pm, gardaí in Donegal Town were faced with two 'violently drunk' youths who were fighting with each other on Quay Street, adjacent to the garda station. Two guards went to break it up and then one of the youths came to the station himself and smashed glass in two doors and kicked another door in the station causing it damage, about €500 worth. "When he was arrested, he dirtied the cell with his own excrement which will cost about €200 to clean," said the guard. The other youth involved in the assault was arrested shortly afterwards for being intoxicated in public. According to the guard both were 'high on drink'.

**Donegal Democrat
13 May 2004**

Activity

1. What sort of problems does alcohol abuse cause (some are highlighted in this article)?

_____

_____

_____

_____

2. What do you think is meant by the chain of causation in law?

_____

_____

_____

3. Do you think that a publican should be responsible for what his/her customers do if they become intoxicated on their premises? Explain your answer.

_____

_____

_____

_____

4. Look through back issues of your local newspaper for articles dealing with alcohol abuse and its effects.

5. Often the media only highlight alcohol abuse and young people. Do you think this is an issue for all age groups? Explain your answer.

_____

_____

_____

Forces and Interests That Affect an Issue

With every issue there are forces and interests at work that affect them for the better or worse. Take alcohol abuse, which was the subject of the last newspaper article.

Some forces that make the issue of alcohol abuse worse are:

- personal problems that cause people to drink to forget them;
- that drinking is seen as part of Irish culture;
- that drunkenness is largely accepted in society;
- that some publicans serve more alcohol to obviously drunk customers.

Some forces that help the issue are:

- self-help groups such as AA, Al Anon and Al Teen;
- addiction counselling services provided free by the health boards;
- alcohol-awareness programmes written for schools.

Interest in the issue

Still taking the issue of alcohol abuse, give your opinion on each of the following questions.

1. Who is affected by this issue?

2. Who is concerned about or interested in the issue?

3. What interest groups or organisations speak out about this issue?

4. Do those most affected by the issue speak out about it? Explain your answer.

5. Who has something to gain by the issue remaining unsolved?

6. Who has something to lose by the issue remaining unsolved?

_____

_____

Activity

Pick an issue; you can, if you like, take it from the list given at the beginning of this module. Identify the forces and interests that affect this issue. Write down your opinions here.

Issue _____

Forces that make the issue worse:

_____

_____

Forces that help the issue:

_____

_____

Who has an interest in leaving the issue unsolved?

_____

_____

Who has something to lose by the issue remaining unsolved?

_____

_____

Key Assignment

Contact an organisation/centre outside school that has information about a contemporary issue. Give a report to your class about what you find out. You may find the list of interest groups in Module 5 on page 207 useful here.

Issue _____

Organisation/Centre

_____

When you have completed this key assignment, go to the beginning of this module and tick it off on the checklist.

Unit 3 *Making Links*

This unit is designed to allow you to make links between various contemporary issues and your everyday life. You will be asked to carry out reading, writing and listening exercises that will help you see how contemporary issues affect you as an individual.

Racism in the Blood

Racism is part of Irish society. If you think that's painful to hear, imagine how painful it is for me to watch and experience. There is no reason why this deeply hurtful oppression need continue in Ireland. Eliminating it, however, will require us to move beyond being morally against it to understanding the real ways it affects our lives and finding the skills to work through it before we tear each other apart.

I have been hit while attending my local bank, stared at, shouted at abusively on the street, told to 'go home', and been ignored queuing in a shop while I watched others behind me be called forward for assistance.

A significant issue here is trust. Racism teaches people in the dominant group they need to be afraid – that the targeted group (Travellers, Muslims, Jews, Africans and Asians) are uncontrollable, untrustworthy and will try to kill them. We act out of fear by blaming them for our problems and keeping them out of our state and our lives.

While many say racism in this state is new, Travellers have been targeted for hundreds of years as violent, drunk, robbing, untrustworthy, cute, abusing the system and dirty. I'm sure you can come up with more.

We are hopelessly focused on the 'others'. For as much as there is a myth that black people want to come to Ireland because it's a wonderful, easy place to live, there are floods of black people leaving this island because it is such a hard place to live when you're black.

Although it is commonly believed that our economic boom brought a dramatic increase in asylum applications in the 1990s, people from Britain, America, Canada and Australia have persistently immigrated to Ireland since the formation of the state. All this time, Ireland refused to provide safety for refugees at all. Only our recent membership of the EU has pressurised us to meet our international obligations to accept and process applications for asylum. Otherwise, we would still keep them out.

While almost everyone is against racism, it takes strength and intelligence to genuinely do something about it.

The Irish Times
23 March 2004

Activity

1. Would you consider yourself to be racist?   Yes ☐   No ☐

2. Do others consider you to be racist?   Yes ☐   No ☐

3. Why, according to the article, are people racist?

_____

_____

_____

4. Case Study: In the past Peter Sweeney has worked on and off as a painter and decorator but has been long-term unemployed for nine years. He lives in a corporation flat in Dublin's North inner city. Peter is extremely racist and frequently shouts abuse at refugees and asylum seekers he meets on the street. It drives him crazy to think that non-nationals are getting welfare benefits or corporation housing.

A. Why do you think Peter is so racist?

_____

_____

_____

B. Do you think Peter has any right to be racist? Explain your answer.

_____

_____

_____

5. In the past Ireland was a very poor country and many people left as economic refugees for countries such as England, America and Australia. What do you think the term economic refugee means?

_____

_____

6. Have you any relations who emigrated as economic refugees because there was no work here?   Yes ☐   No ☐

7. Some people feel that we as a nation should be particularly understanding and sympathetic towards refugees and asylum seekers. Why do you think this should be the case?

_____

_____

_____

8. Comment on the heading given to this article – do you agree with it?

_____

_____

_____

Track 11

Listen to the news item on Track 11 and answer the questions.

1. What two things in this news bulletin would lead you to believe that the young people killed in this accident were joyriders?

A. _____

B. _____

2. Is joyriding a problem in your area?   Yes ☐   No ☐
What are the usual reasons given for young people joyriding?

_____

_____

_____

3. Do you think that these reasons are valid?   Yes ☐   No ☐
Give a reason for your answer.

_____

_____

_____

4. Why do you think some people find it hard to have sympathy for joyriders if they are killed or injured?

_____

_____

5. On a scale of 1-10 how important is the joyriding issue to your daily life? Circle your answer.

1   2   3   4   5   6   7   8   9   10
not relevant at all   extremely relevant

Give a reason for your answer.

_____

_____

_____

Civil war – a contemporary issue

Civil war means 'a war between citizens of the same country' (Oxford Dictionary).

Case study: Rwanda

In 1994 an estimated 1 million people were murdered in Rwanda over a period of 100 days. Why did this happen?

Rwanda is a small, poor African country with a total population of around 8.4 million. The average life expectancy is 41 years. Rwanda is made up of three ethnic groups. The Hutu (85%), the Tutsi (14%) and the Twa (1%). The Tutsi have historically been the wealthier group, owning land, and the Hutu and the Twa working for them. Belgium colonised

Rwanda in 1919 and began educating the Tutsi and giving them positions of authority. This worsened tensions between the Hutu and the Tutsi because it seemed as if the Tutsi were getting everything and the Hutu and the Twa nothing.

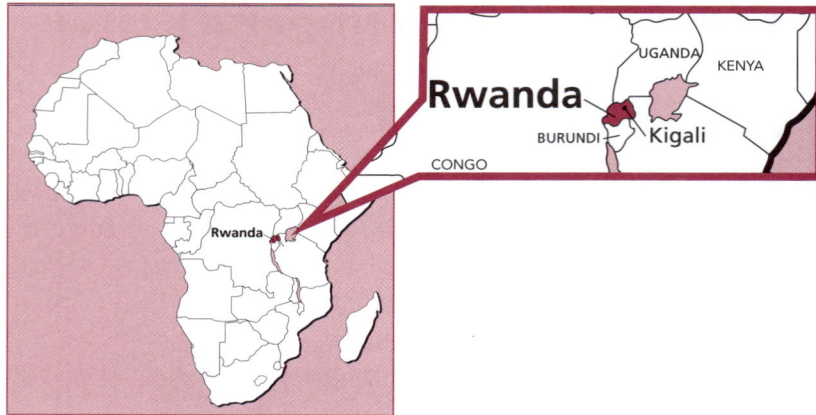

In 1959 the Hutu rebelled and took power, driving many Tutsi out of the country into neighbouring Uganda. Between 1990 and 1993 Tutsi refugees from Uganda returned to Rwanda and began to attack the Hutu. They succeeded in taking over the northern part of Rwanda as their homeland.

On 6 April 1994, however, the Hutu Rwandan president was assassinated. This sparked off a bloody massacre that was to last 100 days and claim over a million lives. Three-quarters of the Tutsi population was killed in a mass genocide. Many countries including France, America, and Belgium suspected the genocide was being planned but did nothing. The United Nations, an organisation set up to prevent atrocities such as this, pulled out of Rwanda shortly before the massacre began.

Activity

1. Find out what the term genocide means.

2. What do you think was the cause of the atrocity in Rwanda?

3. Why do you think the UN pulled out of Rwanda, knowing that a massacre was planned

4. Why do you think countries like France, America and Belgium decided to do nothing about the impending massacre either?

Unit 4 *Contemporary Issues and Human Rights*

The Universal Declaration of Human Rights

Background

On 30 January 1933 Adolf Hitler became leader of Germany. Once in power he and his party called the National Socialists (Nazis) made sure that they took complete control. Hitler made it illegal for newspapers to print anything that went against him or showed him or his party in a bad light. It was illegal to hold meetings or say anything publicly that Hitler didn't approve of. Hitler banned any other political parties and so had total control. He then put together three police forces to keep this control. These forces were called the Gestapo, the SA and the SS.

Miami Holocaust Memorial:
Sculpture of Love and Anguish

Hitler and the Nazi party believed that Germans or the 'Aryan race' were superior to all other races and should take over the world. The Nazis saw Aryans as being typically blond, blue-eyed and tall.

Jews were the first target of the Nazi hate campaign. Jews were not allowed go to cinemas, schools or even walk in certain parts of German cities.

Although the Jews were the main target of German Nazi hate, other groups such as Romas (gypsies), the handicapped and homosexuals were also targeted.

Between 1933 and 1935 Hitler introduced a number of forced sterilisation programmes, whereby thousands of people who the Nazis called 'inferiors' were treated so that they could not have children. Yet worse was to come.

In 1933 the first of Hitler's concentration camps was opened at Dachau, near Munich in Germany. Between this and the end of his reign of terror in 1945 Hitler and his Nazi followers killed a total of 16 million people in these death camps. The biggest of the camps was Auschwitz in Poland, where many thousands were gassed, shot or simply allowed to die of starvation or disease. In some of the camps people were used as human guinea pigs for terrible medical experiments, which often resulted in the death of the person. This reign of terror is known as the Holocaust.

When it was discovered what had gone on in Germany between 1933 and 1945, the Declaration of Human rights was drawn up. It was drawn up by a new organisation called the 'United Nations' to guard against such atrocities ever happening again. The Declaration of Human rights is really a list of rules that explain how we should treat others and how we should expect to be treated in this world. The declaration was passed on 10 December 1948. All members of the United Nations signed the declaration, with eight exceptions – six members of the Soviet bloc, Saudi Arabia and South Africa.

The introduction to the Declaration states that:

'Principals of dignity and equality of all are the foundations of freedom, justice and peace in the world.'

Then 30 articles or statements are given. Below is a summary of them:

1. Everyone is born free and equal and should treat others as they would like to be treated.
2. Nobody should be treated badly because of differences in race, colour, sex, language, religion, etc.
3. Everyone has the right to life, freedom and safety.
4. Nobody should be made a slave.
5. Nobody should suffer cruelty or torture.
6. Everyone must be recognised by the law.
7. Everyone is equal before the law.
8. Everyone has the right to legal representation if their rights are violated.
9. Nobody can be unjustly imprisoned.
10. Everyone has the right to a fair trial.
11. Everyone has the right to be presumed innocent until proven guilty.
12. Everyone has the right to privacy.
13. Everyone has the right to travel within and outside their own country.
14. Everyone has the right to asylum.
15. Everyone has the right to a nationality and to change it.
16. Everyone has the right to marry if of full age.
17. Everyone has the right to own property and for it not to be taken off them.
18. Everyone has the right to freedom of thought, conscience and religion.
19. Everyone has the right to express their opinion without fear of punishment.
20. Everyone has the right to have meetings but not to be forced to join any particular group.
21. Everyone has the right to vote for who they want by secret ballot.

22. Everyone has the right to social security.

23. Everyone has the right to work and to be paid equally for equal work. Everyone has the right to join a trade union.

24. Everyone has the right to leisure time and paid holidays.

25. Everyone has the right to an adequate standard of living with social welfare if you are unable to provide this for yourself.

26. Everyone has the right to a free elementary education.

27. Everyone has the right to enjoy the cultural life of their community.

28. Everyone has the right to social and international order so that these rights can be recognised.

29. The individual is entitled to their human rights once the rights of others are respected at the same time.

30. No country, group or person has the right to take away any of the human rights set out in this declaration.

Key Assignment

Create an A1-sized promotional poster upholding one of the rights in the Universal Declaration of Human Rights.

When you have completed this key assignment, go to the beginning of this module and tick it off on the checklist.

Activity

Read back over the account of the Holocaust and through the articles of the declaration. Can you think of eight rights that were violated by Hitler and his Nazi party during the Holocaust?

1. _____
2. _____
3. _____
4. _____
5. _____
6. _____
7. _____
8. _____

1. Describe briefly what happened in Germany between 1933 and 1945 that caused members of the United Nations to come together and draw up the Declaration of Human Rights.

_____
_____
_____
_____
_____

2. Again in your own words, can you describe what the overall aims or principals of the Declaration are?

_____
_____
_____

3. When was the Declaration signed? _____

4. Some of the rights in the Declaration we take for granted in this country. An example is the right to vote by secret ballot. This right is rarely if ever interfered with nowadays in Ireland. Other rights, however, are still being interfered with. In the space below, write down situations that occur in this country today where people's rights are not being respected. Beside the situation, note which article deals with this right.

Example
Issue _Husband or wife beating_
What rights or articles are relevant to this issue? _Articles 1, 3 and 5_

Issue _____
What rights or articles are relevant to this issue?
_____

Issue _____
What rights or articles are relevant to this issue?
_____

Issue _____
What rights or articles are relevant to this issue?
_____

Types of rights

Now that you are familiar with the articles of the Declaration of Human Rights, you will be able to see that there are different types of rights. These are:

- Political rights
- Social rights
- Cultural rights
- Economic rights

Activity

Show that you know the difference between the various rights by putting them into the correct box. Your teacher may need to help you. The first one has been done for you.

Political rights

Social rights

Article 1

Cultural rights

Economic rights

Exam Time

Social Education (2002) – Long question (part)

1. Look at this picture of Aki, a young child living in poverty somewhere in our world.

From your exploration of the Universal Declaration of Human Rights, choose **two** rights which you think children like Aki are being denied. Give **one** reason why each is an important right.

Right 1 _____

Reason: _____

_____

Right 2 _____

Reason: _____

_____

Unit 5 *Making Connections*

Track 12

Listen to the four news items on Track 12. For each of them, can you write down what human right or rights have been violated? Discuss your answers afterwards.

Item 1 What was the news item about?

_____

What human right or rights were being violated or abused?

_____
_____
_____

Item 2 What was the news item about?

_____

What human right or rights were being violated or abused?

_____
_____
_____

Item 3 What was the news item about?

_____

What human right or rights were being violated or abused?

_____
_____
_____

Item 4 What was the news item about?

_____

What human right or rights were being violated or abused?

_____
_____
_____

Activity

This week make a point of reading a local and a national newspaper and/or watching the news on TV. Pick three issues, one of which is local, one national and one global. Think about each issue in terms of what human rights are under threat.

Local issue _____

Where did you see/read about this issue?

_____

What human rights, if any, are threatened by this issue?

_____

_____

National issue _____

Where did you see/read about this issue?

_____

What human rights, if any, are threatened by this issue

_____

_____

Global issue _____

Where did you see/read about this issue?

_____

What human rights, if any, are threatened by this issue?

_____

_____

Key Assignment

Pick one of the issues that you came across while doing the last activity and that you found particularly interesting. Prepare a small talk to inform your class about it.

When you have completed this key assignment, go to the beginning of this module and tick it off on the checklist.

Key Assignment

Taking the same issue again, or you may choose another one, write down three things that you consider right and three things you consider wrong with regard to this contemporary issue. Explain your ideas to your class. The example may help you.

When you have completed this key assignment, go to the beginning of this module and tick it off on the checklist.

Chosen issue   Refugees coming into this country

Three things right:
1. It is right that everyone is equal regardless of the colour of their skin.
2. It is right that people should be allowed to get out of countries where their lives are in danger.
3. It is right that refugees should be adequately provided for so that they do not have to beg on the streets.

Three things wrong:
1. It is wrong to give abuse to refugees on the street as you do not know anything about them as individuals.
2. It is wrong that applications for asylum take so long to process, which means that the refugee must rely on social welfare.
3. It is wrong that refugees enter the country illegally.

Now your turn:

Chosen issue   _____

Three things right:
1. _____
2. _____
3. _____

Three things wrong:
1. _____
2. _____
3. _____

Unit 6 *Understanding Concepts*

Whenever the issue of human rights is discussed, certain key concepts or ideas usually come up. Below is a list of some of them.

Activity

Match each key concept with its definition. You may need a dictionary to help you.

1. A right _____   A. The unequal treatment of individuals based on age.

2. A responsibility _____   B. The unequal treatment of individuals based on their sex.

3. Democracy _____   C. Calm, quiet and free of disturbances such as war and riots.

4. Human dignity _____   D. The belief that human beings can be divided into races and that some races are inferior to others.

5. Interdependence _____   E. A country ruled by its people.

6. Law _____   F. Taking care of the world's natural resources, e.g. forests.

7. Ageism _____   G. Your duty to others.

8. Health _____   H. Something you are entitled to.

9. Justice _____   I. A group of people who differ in some way from the most common group in a society.

10. Sexism _____   J. The most powerful group in a society.

11. Racism _____   K. Having respect for others.

12. Prejudice _____   L. A state of physical, mental and social well-being.

13. Peace _____   M. Nations or people depending on each other.

14. Equality _____   N. The rules which try to control society.

15. Dominant group _____   O. Fairness

---

16. Safety	___	P. An opinion formed without full knowledge.
19. Minority groups	___	Q. To be treated the same.
20. Poverty	___	R. Free from danger.
21. Environmental protection	___	S. In need, without enough.

Activity

Sometimes a contemporary issue arises where there is a conflict of rights. Look at the three situations below. Can you see that both sides have rights even though they conflict?

Situation 1
Rumours have been circulating around a small town that a certain man, let's call him Mr X, has raped and beaten a number of young girls and women in the local area. A group of people call on Mr X's home and beat him to within an inch of his life.

Explain how there is a conflict of rights:

_____
_____
_____

Situation 2
A company owned by a man called Mr Y declares itself bankrupt and does not pay its debts to a number of people who have invested their life savings in it. Mr Y says that he cannot honour the debts. The people who are owed the money see that Mr. Y lives in a big house and seems to be very well off. They want him to be forced to sell his house and pay them back their money.

Explain how there is a conflict of rights:

_____
_____
_____

Situation 3
A second class teacher in a primary school refuses to have one particular boy in her class. The teacher claims that the boy is so disruptive that the other children in the class learn very little

when he is there. Most days the boy is sent out of class and spends his time looking at the pictures in magazines. The boy cannot read.

Explain how there is a conflict of rights:

_____

_____

_____

Watch one or more of the following films. Each of these films deals with examples of the violation of human rights.

Schindler's List   *Not Without my Daughter*
Saving Private Ryan   *The Thin Red Line*
The Colour Purple   *To Kill a Mocking Bird*
Amistad   *In the Name of the Father*
Murder in the First   *Philadelphia*
Mississippi Burning

Summarise what the film is about and what human rights you think were violated in the film.

_____

_____

_____

_____

_____

_____

_____

_____

_____

_____

_____

_____

_____

_____

_____

_____

_____

_____

A Contemporary Issue Investigated:
Irish Travellers and Human Rights

Irish Travellers are a native minority group who have been part of Irish society for many centuries. Traveller culture is a separate and definite one. It has its own value systems, language, customs and traditions, which are very different from those of the settled community.

Irish Travellers, like European Roma and Gypsies, share the common experience of social exclusion and discrimination. All of these groups have had to fight hard to keep their separate identity and culture. They have had to resist or stop attempts by the settled community to try to make them conform to what is considered 'normal'. In this section we

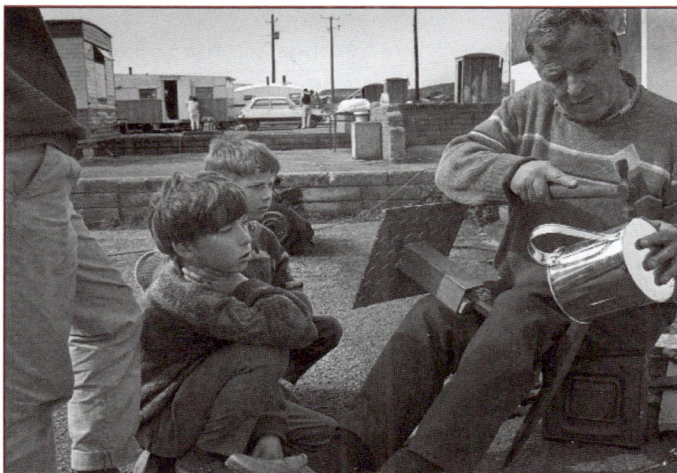

Many traditional traveller trades are now gone, leaving many unemployed.

will look at the Traveller issue from a human rights perspective. You will be asked to think hard about your own attitudes to this, our largest minority group.

What it is to be a Traveller

Irish Travellers, of whom there are an estimated 23,681 (Census 2002) living in this country, are a people with a separate identity and culture. The Irish Traveller is as fully Irish as the majority population but comes from a separate minority ethnic group.

An ethnic group is a group that has each of the following characteristics:
- a long, shared history;
- a shared, distinct set of customs and traditions;
- a common ancestry;
- a separate language(s).

The Irish Traveller certainly displays all of the above characteristics.

Traveller history, although largely unreported, can be traced back to the twelfth century. The customs and traditions of Travellers are largely related to the tradition of nomadism. Nomadism means travelling as a way of life. Nomadic people have a different attitude to place than the settled community.

A common ancestry means being born into a certain group. One must be born a Traveller; you cannot just decide to become a Traveller. (New age travellers are members of the settled community who decide to lead a similar life to the traditional Traveller. They are not part of the Irish Traveller ethnic group.)

Irish Travellers have their own language called the Cant, Gammon or Shelta. It is a distinct language in itself and has a long history.

Frequently, minority ethnic groups are the subject of discrimination and oppression. The Irish Traveller as a minority ethnic group is no exception. Many people see the Irish Traveller as a problem, the solution to which is integrating them into the general population. When the Traveller issue was first addressed by the Irish government in the 1960s, its policy was to, 'promote their absorption into the general community' (Commission on Itinerancy, 1963).

Some facts about Travellers

Health

Travellers are only now reaching the life expectancy that settled Irish people achieved in the 1940s.

Male Travellers die on average 10 years before settled males.

Female Travellers die on average 12 years before settled females.

Only 5% of Travellers live to be 50 years old and only 2% live to be 65.

Infant mortality rates (the number of Traveller babies dying) is nearly three times that of the settled community.

(Economic and Social Research Unit)

Accommodation

40% of Travellers (1,149 families) still live by the side of the road on unofficial sites, subject to the constant fear of eviction.

48% of Travellers have no access to piped water.

50% of Travellers have no access to a toilet.

55% of Travellers have no electricity.

50% of all Travellers live in Dublin, Galway, Limerick and Cork.

(Economic and Social Research Unit)

Education

Only 50% of Traveller children under 12 years attend school.

80% of Travellers between the ages of 12 and 15 do not attend school.

There are very high rates of illiteracy among Travellers.

(Economic and Social Research Unit)

Traveller discrimination from a human-rights perspective

The circumstances of the Irish Travelling People are intolerable. No humane and decent society, once made aware of such circumstances, could permit them to persist.

(Economic and Social Research Institute, 1986)

We are not unique in refusing to acknowledge the existence of racism and breaches of human rights in our own country. Like many other countries, especially in Europe, we tend to see these breaches as being a problem in some far off land. We refuse to see them in ourselves or in our own country. In addition there is a tendency to see racism only in terms of skin colour, so it is frequently said that Travellers cannot experience racism because they are white, and are not a different race nor a different nationality.

Activity

1. Can you think of four human rights that are frequently denied to Travellers in this country?

A. _____

B. _____

C. _____

D. _____

2. Why do you think that Travellers die younger than members of the settled community?

_____

_____

3. Why do you think so few Traveller children go to school beyond the age of 12 years?

_____

_____

4. Why do you think there are such high levels of unemployment among Travellers?

_____

_____

5. If you were a member of the Government what would you do to improve Travellers' lives?

_____

_____

_____

_____

6. It has often been said that discrimination against Travellers is getting worse rather than better. Why do you think this is?

_____

_____

_____

7. Absorbing or assimilating Travellers into the settled community is not the answer.

Do you agree with this statement?   Yes ☐   No ☐

Explain your answer:

_____

_____

_____

_____

_____

_____

_____

Knockcroghery Houses Vandalised

Two new houses in the Knockcroghery area, which were purchased by Roscommon County Council for Traveller accommodation, were vandalised over the weekend, but the Traveller family due to move into one of the properties have since vowed to remain in their new home.

The two four-bedroomed bungalows located at Cornamart, Knockcroghery were vandalised on Friday and Saturday night last, when the windows in both houses were smashed.

It is understood that Martin and Margaret Mongan from Roscommon town were due to move into one of the houses but were not present when the house was attacked. There is now growing speculation that that vandalism was motivated by opposition to Travellers moving into the Knockcroghery area.

Roscommon Gardaí are currently investigating the incident. The two new, vacant houses were purchased by Roscommon County Council under the Traveller Accommodation Programme and one of the houses was allocated to a Traveller family recently.

Fianna Fáil local election candidate in Mid-Roscommon, Paddy Kilduff, has called on Roscommon County Council to give priority to people from the Knockcroghery area on the housing list saying: "I am calling on Roscommon County Council to house the people in St John's, Lecarrow and Knockcroghery area on the housing list. I know of some people on the housing list for the past seven or eight years and I am calling for people in the area to be given priority for housing rather than bringing people out from Roscommon town."

It is understood that a total of eight windows in the house were smashed and will now have to be reordered. Mr Mongan, his wife and nine children are since understood to have moved into the house and are determined to make their home in the area.

Martin Mongan is a member of the Travelling community and is a native of Roscommon. He and his wife and children have been living in a caravan on the Circular Road, Roscommon, for the last two and half years.

Roscommon Herald
28 April 2004

Activity

1. Why do you think the houses were vandalised, and what do you think the vandals hoped to achieve by their actions?

_____

_____

_____

2. Had these houses being allocated to non-Traveller families from Roscommon town do you think the vandalism would have occurred? Explain your answer.

_____

_____

_____

3. How do you think Mr. Mongan and his family feel about what happened?

_____

_____

_____

5. What provision is there for Traveller families in your area, for example a halt site?

_____

_____

Key Assignment

For this key assignment you must take part in a roleplay (either as a participant or an observer) where a denial of human rights is at issue. You must write down what you observed during the roleplay afterwards and keep this in your Social Education folder as evidence of assignments completed.

When you have completed this key assignment, go to the beginning of this module and tick it off on the checklist.

Ideas for roleplays

Immigrants
Roleplays may address how society at large sees immigrants; how you as an individual see immigrants; begging; solutions to the issues raised.

Unemployment
Roleplays may address why unemployment is still a problem with the economy doing so well; what groups most frequently face unemployment; the taxpayers' view of unemployment; people with employment claiming benefit and keeping it secret; solutions to the issues raised.

Sexual harassment
Roleplays may address what is meant by sexual harassment; sexual harassment in the workplace; around your peers; whether the harassers are aware of who they are; how sexual harassment be best dealt with.

Racism
Roleplays may address reasons for racism; who is racist; how do people show their racist tendencies; solutions to the issues raised.

Discrimination (class, sex, sexual orientation, religion)
Roleplays may address your own experiences of discrimination; who you as an individual discriminate against; who society as a whole discriminates against and why.

Disability
Roleplays may address problems with travel; work; how society sees disability; how you view disability; whether the benefits available are good enough; whether disabled people are treated as equals; solutions to the issues raised.

Key Assignment

Throughout this chapter you have looked at many different contemporary issues. With other members of your class organise a survey on attitudes in your local area to a particular issue.

When you have completed this key assignment, go to the beginning of this module and tick it off on the checklist.

Module 4

Social and Health Education 2

This module should be completed during sessions 3 and 4 (Year 2).

Below are the four key assignments for Module 4. You must do ALL of these. As you work through this module and complete each one, come back to this page and tick it off.

1. As a member of a group I have made a list/chart/collage or picture of appropriate ways of dealing with feelings of anger.

    Date: _____

2. I have described a method that I have used, either in real life or in roleplay, in trying to solve a conflict situation or in dealing with criticism.

    Date: _____

3. I have listed the main tasks and responsibilities involved each day in taking care of:
    • a three-month-old baby, or
    • a three-year-old child, or
    • a ten-year-old child.

    Date: _____

4. I have listed the agencies that help with a particular health or addiction problem and identified the sort of help they provide. I have described ways of contacting these agencies and accessing help and advice.

    Date: _____

Unit 1 *Communication*

To be happy in our lives and to be able to form lasting relationships with others we need to understand and be able to express our feelings. An inability to do this causes feelings to build up inside over time. This causes stress and sometimes a reliance on alcohol or other drugs in an effort to cope.

Many physical and mental illnesses are linked to stress, some of which are heart disease, high blood pressure, headaches, ulcers and depression.

Up to a certain age children are generally allowed to express their feelings freely. They can cry or have tantrums whenever they feel annoyed or frustrated and nobody really expects them to control themselves. Later, though, society and the people around us tell us that certain feelings need to be suppressed or kept inside. This can be very harmful to us. While it is essential that we control how we express our feelings, for example you cannot just lash out and hit someone who is annoying you, it is not good to ignore our feelings altogether. Our feelings should be released in a safe way that respects the people around us.

This unit will help you to identify and name different feelings and emotions and learn ways to express them in an appropriate and healthy way.

Activity

Name all the feelings you can think of, both emotional and physical, in the box below.

From the list that you have written in the box, group them into feelings that are physical and feelings that are emotional on the next page.

Physical	**Emotional**

Now group the feelings into those that are positive or good and those that are negative and can harm you if they are not expressed appropriately.

Positive	**Negative**

Pick three feelings that you listed under positive and three feelings you listed under negative. Write an example of a recent situation when you experienced each of the feelings listed. You might like to discuss what you have written in small groups.

Note: Do not write down any information in the following two exercises if you do not feel comfortable doing so.

Three positive feelings

1. Name of feeling _____
   Recent situation _____

2. Name of feeling _____
   Recent situation _____

3. Name of feeling _____
   Recent situation _____

Three negative feelings

1. Name of feeling _____
   Recent situation _____

2. Name of feeling _____
   Recent situation _____

3. Name of feeling _____
   Recent situation _____

As can be seen above there are certain feelings that we call positive feelings and certain others that we call negative feelings. Negative feelings are generally caused when the facts of a situation get changed by us into negative beliefs. For example if you fail an exam, a negative belief would be 'I failed an exam so I must be stupid'.

Activity

Fill out the work card below. Note to yourself what negative beliefs are at work when you experience a negative feeling.

I feel/felt proud when:

_____
_____

I feel/felt down when:

_____
_____

I feel/felt nervous or worried when:

_____
_____

I feel/felt angry when:

_____
_____

I feel/felt happy when:

_____
_____

I feel/felt awkward or embarrassed when:

_____

_____

I feel/felt afraid when:

_____

_____

Anger and Aggression and How to Deal with It

Anger is perhaps the most destructive emotion if it is kept inside and not expressed. Keeping anger inside can cause emotional and behavioural problems. In our society, though, expression of our anger in an aggressive way is not acceptable. This is necessary for social order and safety. If society permitted us to go around beating up everyone that made us angry, life would be very difficult for all of us.

What everyone must try to do is learn to control their anger. It is OK to get angry; the important thing is not to lose your temper and become verbally or physically abusive or violent. Instead explain to the person you are angry with as calmly as you can why it is you are angry with them.

If someone else is angry with you, there is often not a lot you can do about it. Let them have their say, without interrupting them. A lot of the time it is pointless trying to reason with them when they are in the middle of their angry outburst. You may even start to lose your temper yourself. This will end up with both of you going away feeling terrible.

Tips for dealing with your anger

- Get rid of the tension caused by your anger – run, go for a walk, do breathing exercises, write down why you are angry, punch a cushion.
- Tell the person calmly why you are angry with them.
- Listen to what they have to say.
- Work out together what you can both do about the situation.

Receiving criticism

Criticism can be either constructive or destructive. Constructive criticism is not given to put us down or make us feel small but to help us learn and improve. Destructive criticism on the other hand is negative in nature and is not designed to help us. People who constantly put others down in this way are often unhappy with themselves and think that if they can put others down they will feel better about themselves. Of course they never do; if you put down others, it will only make you feel worse.

Destructive criticism

From time to time we all come across people who are very critical of others. They make hurtful remarks, which are not designed to help us in any way but designed to try to make us feel bad. If someone treats you like this, the best idea is to ignore what is being said and try to avoid getting angry.

Constructive criticism

Constructive criticism is when someone offers their opinion to us or gives us suggestions for improvements. Constructive criticism is frequently asked for, it is not designed to hurt us but to help us. Some people however have difficulty dealing with any kind of criticism, even constructive criticism. They see all forms of criticism as a put-down and often get very angry and defensive.

Activity

Look at the situation below. Which of the two teachers is trying to give constructive criticism?

Teacher A ☐   Teacher B ☐

Situation   A student hands up an English essay. He is not very good at English. The teacher makes the following remarks when she is giving back the essay.

Teacher A	'Do you think I have nothing better to be at with my evenings than correcting this rubbish?'
Teacher B	'Seamus, this essay as it is would not pass. You need to work on putting some sort of order on your essays. You won't be able to do this over night, but you can make a start. For tomorrow write an interesting opening paragraph. Try to grab the reader's attention.'

Dealing with criticism

- Think about whether the criticism is valid or invalid. Is it meant to be constructive?

- If it is invalid, it is best to stay calm and either ignore what has been said or tell the person that what they have said has hurt you.

- If the criticism is valid, think about how you can learn from it.

Activity

List three personal criticisms that you have received recently.

1. _____
2. _____
3. _____

Were they constructive criticisms?
1. Yes ☐   No ☐
2. Yes ☐   No ☐
3. Yes ☐   No ☐

How did you feel in each of the situations?
1. _____
2. _____
3. _____

How did you deal with the criticism in each situation?
1. _____
2. _____
3. _____

Key Assignment

In groups of two (or three if you include an observer) choose one of the following roleplays, or one of your own. You may like to deal badly with some of the criticisms, just to highlight the difference between this and dealing well with criticism.

When you have completed this key assignment, go to the beginning of this module and tick it off on the checklist.

Roleplay 1 You tog out for leisure and recreation class and a member of your group starts criticising what you have on and how you look.

Roleplay 2 You have done a rough copy of your first task and your teacher is going through it with you. She is giving you constructive criticism.

Roleplay 3 You are going out on your first work experience to a solicitor's office and come into school beforehand dressed in a tracksuit. Your work experience teacher does not think you are dressed very appropriately and offers you some suggestions about what it would be better to wear.

Roleplay 4 You are going out on a Saturday night and have on a very revealing outfit. Your father takes one look at the outfit and starts criticising how you look.

Roleplay 5 You are playing a football/basketball match and things are not going too well. The coach gives you a lecture at half time about what you are doing wrong.

Key Assignment

For this key assignment you are required to describe a method of trying to solve conflicts.

Complete the activities below and then roleplay them.

When you have completed this key assignment, go to the beginning of this module and tick it off on the checklist.

Place yourself in the following situations. Write down how each of the people in them could effectively control their anger, yet not passively accept the wrongs that have been done to them:

Sarah

Sarah, who is 17 years old, has been going out with Sean, who is 18, for the past four months. Today at school Mary, a fairly close friend, told Sarah that a girl in another class was seen with Sean at the weekend after the disco. Mary is fairly sure that the information is reliable and that Sean has therefore been cheating on Sarah. Sarah is furious. She cannot believe what she is hearing.

What do you think Sarah should do?_____

_____

What should Sarah not do? _____

_____

Patrick

During maths class Niall throws a rolled-up ball of paper at the teacher when his back is turned. The teacher opens out the ball of paper and sees that it is Patrick's work. The teacher automatically assumes that Patrick is responsible for throwing the ball of paper, and says that Patrick is to report to detention after school. Patrick is not very good at maths and frequently causes trouble in this class. However, this occasion is different as Patrick was for once trying to do his work when the missile was thrown.

What do you think Patrick should do? _____

_____

What should Patrick not do? _____

_____

Joan

Joan is 16 years old. Her parents are very strict compared to most of the parents of the other girls in her class. They have refused to let her go out on a Saturday night to an over-18s club in the town. Joan thinks that this is very unfair and that they are just trying to spoil the fun for her. Joan is going mad as it is nearly 10 o'clock and everyone is meeting at 10.30.

What do you think Joan should do? _____

_____

What should Joan not do? _____

_____

Real-life situation
Can you think of a time when you were involved in a conflict
situation with someone? Write an account of what happened and
how you dealt with the anger you felt.

_____
_____
_____
_____
_____
_____
_____
_____

Decisions! Decisions!

Every day each one of us makes many decisions. Most of these decisions do not have
long-term consequences and therefore we make them quickly without thinking too much.
Examples of these decisions are what to wear or what to have for our breakfast. Other
decisions, however, have long-term consequences and therefore require a good deal of
thought before being made.

How decisions are made

Put it off
This is when you decide not to make a decision. The problem that
needs to be solved never gets solved if you choose this option.

Follow others
This is when you allow peer pressure or other things like advertising
to influence your decision. You make your decision based on what
everyone else is doing.

Act on impulse/
gut feeling
This is when you do not consciously think about the decision at all,
but you follow your instincts alone. For example, you grab a child
before he or she runs out in front of an oncoming car.

Play it safe This is when you choose the option that carries with it no risk. An example would be you decide not to apply to any colleges in case you do not like living away from home.

Think through Generally this is the best method to choose when deciding important matters that have long-term effects. Using this method you weigh up the pros and cons and make your decision based on this.

Activity

What decision-making methods do you think each person used in the following situations?

Case 1
Eddie and four of his friends hang around the back of the shopping centre on Saturday nights. Last Saturday Paul had some hash and made a few joints out of it. Eddie had never smoked hash before but decided to smoke some of it.

Case 2
Sean has been going out with Paula for five months now. Over the past few weeks he has gone off Paula a bit and doesn't really want to go out with her anymore. He hasn't broken it off though as he knows she'll be upset and he hates that sort of hassle.

Case 3
Jacinta has a young child called Brian, who is two years old. Brian pulls down a stack of CDs from a shelf in the sitting room. Jacinta slaps Brian in the heat of the moment.

Case 4
Debbie is 18 years old and is finishing her Leaving Certificate Applied next June. Debbie has approached the career guidance teacher for advice about careers. The careers teacher assessed her and told Debbie that her interests seem to lie in creative careers. Debbie decides to apply to three different courses in Dublin, namely interior design, fashion design and drama.

Unit 2 *Relationships*

Types of Relationships

Throughout our lives we are constantly involving ourselves in relationships with other people. These relationships have different functions and we behave differently in each of them according to their function. We form close, loving relationships with family and friends and more formal, functional relationships with people like teachers, doctors and work mates. For any relationship to be successful there must be give and take. In this section we are going to focus on loving relationships and look at what we as people give to them and gain from them.

Activity

Think of one loving or personal relationship in your life at the moment. Name that relationship below and then write down what you want from that relationship and what you can give to that relationship. You could focus on your relationship with a parent, sibling, boyfriend or girlfriend.

Relationship _____

Name three things you want from that relationship:

1. _____
2. _____
3. _____

Name three things that you can give to that relationship:

1. _____
2. _____
3. _____

Not all relationships are as close as this; other relationships may be more superficial or not as deep. You have a relationship with a huge number of different people throughout your day. Examples include shopkeepers and school maintenance staff. Can you think of three such relationships?

1. _____
2. _____
3. _____

Skills for Healthy Relationships

Activity

Hidden in the word search are 15 skills for healthy relationships. Can you find them?

```
U  N  D  E  R  S  T  A  N  D  I  N  G
C  D  D  F  M  G  R  P  Z  X  Y  N  E
C  E  M  P  A  T  H  Y  F  G  R  N  N
O  P  A  R  Q  A  A  B  D  L  F  W  U
O  E  D  O  N  C  T  R  U  S  T  K  I
P  N  M  Y  E  J  L  F  H  M  S  I  N
E  D  I  M  T  P  P  Y  U  Y  S  N  E
R  A  R  S  F  L  T  R  M  B  M  D  S
A  B  A  A  E  S  U  M  O  U  R  N  S
T  L  T  H  E  S  D  L  U  A  E  E  S
I  E  I  N  M  D  V  D  R  Q  S  S  L
O  M  O  E  D  P  L  N  F  F  P  S  C
N  H  N  Q  C  O  N  F  I  D  E  N  T
M  E  F  A  I  T  H  F  U  L  C  F  C
C  O  M  P  A  S  S  I  O  N  T  E  C
```

1. _____	2. _____	3. _____
4. _____	5. _____	6. _____
7. _____	8. _____	9. _____
10. _____	11. _____	12. _____
13. _____	14 _____	15. _____

Discuss what each word means in terms of relationships.

Activity

All relationships, with the possible exception of your family, must be started. Every relationship, including your relationship with your family, must then be maintained and sometimes relationships must be ended. Each of these stages are the subject of a letter on the problem page below. Give some sound advice to the letter writers.

dearTina

Dear Tina,

I have a Saturday job packing shelves in my local supermarket. I really fancy a guy who works there. He hasn't really spoken much to me yet, but has smiled at me a few times. I have a feeling he fancies me as well.

What should I do next?

Yours
Sarah

Dear Sarah

_____

_____

_____

_____

_____

_____

_____

Dear Tina,

I have been going out with a lovely girl for the past three weeks. The problem is I am afraid she'll dump me. I have had other relationships but have never been able to maintain them for very long. The trouble is I tend to get too possessive and then the girl starts saying she feels trapped. I really want this relationship to work as I think I love this girl. Can you help?

Yours
Alan

Dear Alan

_____

_____

_____

_____

_____

_____

_____

Dear Tina,

I have a 'friend'. Let's call her Anna. She is always running me down. She borrows everything belonging to me including my fellas! She tries to make me look stupid in front of others by making me the butt of her jokes. The trouble is I have known Anna since I was in national school and she does have some good points. Should I end this friendship and if so how?

Yours
Ellen

Dear Ellen

_____

_____

_____

_____

_____

_____

_____

Family Structures

Over the last few decades the structure of Irish families has changed. Research and write about each of the family structures listed below.

- Traditional nuclear family

- Extended family

- Lone-parent family

- Blended family

- Families headed by gay or lesbian couples

- Institutions (children's homes, convents, etc)

- Mixed-race family

Track 13

Some young people, for whatever reason, do not live with their families. Every year children who are considered at risk are removed from their families and taken into care by the health boards. In the past, children's homes were very harsh places. Children were made to work long hours and discipline was very strict. Today, children's homes are much improved. This is not to say that life in care is always pleasant.

Listen to the case study on Track 13. What does the speaker find most difficult about being in care?

Becoming a Parent

Becoming a parent can be one of the most rewarding experiences in a person's life. Some psychologists believe that to reproduce is in fact essential to a person's feelings of having led a useful life, and that people who do not have children always feel that they have missed out on something. Having said this, every year children are removed by social services from their natural parent(s), because they are feared to be at risk from serious physical or psychological injury. For this reason, potential parents must be aware of the responsibilities that becoming a parent brings with it.

Babies bring both great joy and great responsibility.

Responsibilities before and during pregnancy

It is the duty of every couple planning to have a baby to give him or her every chance of being born healthy and well. For the pregnant woman in particular this may involve certain changes in lifestyle and diet.

Diet during pregnancy

A woman's diet during pregnancy not only affects a woman's health but the health of her baby. Poor diet during pregnancy has been linked with conditions such as spina bifida and other abnormalities. It is, therefore, the responsibility of every pregnant woman to ensure that she has a balanced diet during pregnancy.

Smoking

It is the responsibility of every woman and her partner, if they smoke, to stop smoking if they decide to have a baby. Sometimes the woman stops and the man doesn't, thinking that his smoking has no effect on the unborn baby. This is untrue; passive smoking harms the baby in much the same way. Besides men should show encouragement and support for the woman by breaking their own smoking habits. Smoking during pregnancy causes the placenta to become less efficient, thus depriving the baby of oxygen. Babies of smokers are more likely to be miscarried and if not may suffer in the following ways:

- be smaller and weaker;
- be premature;
- be a victim of cot death in the first months of life;
- have breathing difficulties, e.g. asthma.

Alcohol

Studies on animals show that heavy drinking by either parent can effect the unborn baby. Male mice injected with alcohol before mating are more likely to father babies that die in the womb. It seems possible, therefore, that some human miscarriages may be related to the heavy drinking of the baby's father before conception.

Foetal alcohol syndrome is a condition that effects babies of women who drink while pregnant. Babies born with this condition suffer various degrees of physical and mental handicap. There are a yet no safe guidelines for alcohol consumption during pregnancy, so the usual advice is to stop drinking altogether.

Other drugs

Marijuana, cocaine, LSD, heroin and glue sniffing all effect foetal development, especially the development of the brain. Babies may suffer withdrawal symptoms at birth. It is the responsibility of drug misusers to seek help for their drug habits before conceiving a baby.

When the baby is born

When a baby is born it depends on its parent(s) for everything. Babies need someone to be there for them 24 hours a day. The parents' social life must therefore be seriously curtailed. Nights out become rare. Continuing full-time education can be very difficult; childcare is very expensive and grandparents may be unable or unwilling to take on the responsibility of a small baby.

The cost of a baby

Babies are very costly. Many couples do not realise this until after the baby is born. For the average couple on an average income a baby means making many sacrifices. Spending on non-essential items such as entertainment, hobbies and non-essential clothing has to be vastly reduced. Some people may have no income other than that provided by the state. Providing adequately for a baby on welfare alone can be a very difficult task.

Responsibility for a child's emotional well-being

How a child develops emotionally and socially is hugely affected by what he or she experiences in the home. It is every parent's responsibility to provide a safe, stable and secure environment for a child to grow up in. Ideally, parents need to be confident that they can provide this environment for a child before having one. Routine is important in a young child's life in order to feel secure.

Helping your child reach his or her full potential

Babies and toddlers are very eager to learn about the world around them. It is a parent's responsibility to provide a stimulating environment for them. Parents should try to read with their child, play games, listen to him or her, go for walks, etc. When a child begins school, it is the parents' responsibility to support their child's learning at home. Parents who have problems themselves with reading and writing may find helping their child with school work a daunting task. To redress this, many early school leavers return to education when they have young children of their own.

Activity

Invite a young parent to visit your group to speak about their experiences. You will have to prepare for the visit very well. Make a list of all the questions you would like to ask beforehand.

Activity

The cost of a baby
Price the following essential items in shops in your area.

1 medium-priced cot	_____
1 medium-priced pram	_____
1 medium-priced car seat/carry cot	_____
1 bottle steriliser (even if breast feeding)	_____
2 medium-priced toys	_____
3 cot blankets	_____
2 sets cot sheets	_____
10 baby vests	_____
10 babygrows	_____
2 snowsuits (or outfits suitable for outside)	_____
3 baby cardigans	_____
6 bottles	_____
4 pkts newborn nappies	_____
Total cost:	_____

Note: This is a shopping list for a baby in the first weeks of life; more expense will follow as the baby gets older. If you already have a baby, maybe you could write about your experience instead of completing the next exercise.

Would you be prepared to...?

		Yes	No	Don't know
1.	Give up smoking?	☐	☐	☐
2.	Give up alcohol before and during pregnancy? (if you are male, reduce your intake in support of your partner)	☐	☐	☐
3.	Reduce nights out to 1-2 per month?	☐	☐	☐
4.	Put your education on hold?	☐	☐	☐
5.	Get up 3-4 times per night to feed the baby?	☐	☐	☐
6.	Never lose your temper even if you are tired or irritated?	☐	☐	☐
7.	Reduce your spending to essentials?	☐	☐	☐
8.	Take responsibility for someone else for the next 18 years?	☐	☐	☐
9.	Do you have the financial means to provide for a baby?	☐	☐	☐
10.	Would you be able to offer a baby a stable environment?	☐	☐	☐
11.	Would you feel confident enough to support your child's education?	☐	☐	☐
12.	Would you have the support of family and friends if you or your girlfriend were to have a baby?	☐	☐	☐

Key Assignment

For this key assignment you must list the main tasks involved in taking care of:
- a three-month-old baby;
- a three-year-old child;
- a ten-year-old child.

Many of the main tasks are listed in the box below. Pick out the tasks relevant to each of the different-aged children and write them in the space provided under each. Some tasks may be relevant to more than one age group.

When you have completed this key assignment, go to the beginning of this module and tick it off on the checklist.

Sterilising bottles   Drying clothes   Tidying up toys

Preparing finger foods   Winding

Supervising bath time   Changing nappies   Making packed lunches

Helping with homework   Washing clothes

Making up bottles   Supervising toy clean-up

Reminding to wash teeth   School collection

Bringing to school   Breast feeding   Top and toe bath

Reading picture books   Four-hourly feeds

Making breakfast   Involving child in housework

Helping child with toileting   Helping to wash teeth

Three-month-old baby

_____
_____
_____
_____
_____

Three-year-old child

_____
_____
_____
_____
_____

Ten-year-old child

_____
_____
_____
_____

Rights and Responsibilities in the Home

Often fights or arguments in the home arise out of a conflict of rights between parents and their children. As a young person you are probably more aware of your own rights than those of your parents.

Activity

Here are some examples of conflicts. What rights do parents have in these situations?

1. You feel you have the right to have your friends over any time.

Your parent(s) feel: _____

2. You feel you shouldn't have to do much work around the house. After all you don't get paid for it.

Your parent(s) feel: _____

3. You feel you have the right to stay home from school.

Your parent(s) feel: _____

4. You feel you have the right to stay over at your boyfriend's or girlfriend's house.

Your parent(s) feel: _____

Problems in Families

From time to time problems arise in every family. When a problem occurs in a family, it is usual that everyone is affected by it even though it may seem to involve only one or two members. As a class, try to think of as many family problems as possible. Write five of the ones you came up with.

1. _____
2. _____
3. _____
4. _____
5. _____

For each of the problems that you have listed find out the name of either a statutory (government-run) or voluntary organisation that can help with the problem.

1. _____
2. _____
3. _____
4. _____
5. _____

Activity

Read the article below which deals with poverty, a common problem in Irish families.

Celtic Tragedy

250,000 Irish kids are living on the breadline and are denied basic rights

One in four Irish children are living in poverty, it was revealed yesterday. A report by the Combat Poverty Agency (CPA) shows that despite the booming economy, falling unemployment and rising incomes, 250,000 children come from poor homes. Agency director Hugh Frazer said poorer children are denied their basic rights and are at serious risk of suffering poor health because their parents earn less than half the average income.

He said, 'by allowing child poverty to continue in this country, we are denying over a quarter of a million children their basic rights to fulfil their talents and potential. How children live today powerfully influences how they live tomorrow. Poverty has negative effects on the health and development of children. Those who grow up in poverty are less likely to do well educationally, have fewer recreational, social and cultural opportunities, and are more at risk of being involved in anti-social behaviour'.

In a recent UNICEF survey of the world's 23 richest countries, Ireland was ranked sixth worst in child poverty levels with 17% of children living below the bread line. There are twice as many poor children in Ireland than in Holland or France, and we have six times more children living below the bread line than in Scandinavia. Mr Frazer said that, 'Ireland no longer has any excuse for these shocking poverty levels. He said that we are in a unique position in our history, in that we now have the resources and the capacity to end the scandal of children being raised in poverty.'

The challenge is to develop public policies which will redistribute these resources in favour of children on the lowest incomes. End child poverty – we can well afford it was the message of a group of children who marched to Dublin Castle yesterday to highlight the issue.

The latest study also revealed the shocking news that one in six children are living in 'extreme' poverty. In this least well-off bracket youngsters go without dinner or breakfast and miss out on school trips.

Irish children who come from unemployed parents are

at much greater risk of poverty. Sixty per cent of poorer children have parents who are out of work.

The CPA hopes to completely abolish child poverty by 2020. Tackling the problem through reforms in child income support is the most effective measure according to Hugh Frazer. The poverty watchdog estimates that it would cost €650 million a year over a three-year period to restructure child welfare payments.

The Mirror

1. How many Irish children come from poor homes? _____

2. Why is it surprising in this day and age in Ireland that there is so much poverty?

_____

_____

_____

3. 'The poverty trap' is a common phrase used when talking about poverty. Why are children brought up in poverty likely to be poor themselves as adults?

_____

_____

_____

4. What agency mentioned in this article is concerned with tackling the problem of poverty?

_____

5. Do you think that increasing social welfare payments is the solution to this problem? Give a reason for your answer.

Yes ☐   No ☐

_____

_____

_____

Family Conflict

Sources of conflict in the home

Listen to the scenes on Tracks 14, 15 and 16. Each of them depicts a family conflict situation. Answer the questions that follow.

Scene 1 (Track 14)

1. What rule did Siobhan's parent(s) set for her? Do you think it is fair? Explain your answer.

_____

_____

_____

2. How would you describe Siobhan's attitude to her parents during this conversation?

_____

_____

_____

3. What reasons does Siobhan give for staying out late and for drinking?

_____

_____

_____

4. On the whole, do you think that Siobhan's parents handled this situation well? Explain your answer.

_____

_____

_____

5. If you were one of Siobhan's parents, what would you do in this situation?

_____

_____

_____

Scene 2 (Track 15)

1. What two reasons does Joan give for not wanting to go to school?

_____

_____

2. How would you describe Joan's mother's behaviour?

Passive ☐   Assertive ☐   Aggressive ☐

3. Do you think that Joan's mother was right to give Joan an ultimatum – that she had go to school every day or get herself a job? Explain your answer.

_____

_____

_____

4. Do you think Joan treats her mother with respect? Explain your answer.

_____

_____

_____

5. What would you do if you were Joan's mother?

_____

_____

_____

Scene 3 (Track 16)

1. Do you think that it is the responsibility of every young person living at home to do their share of housework? Explain your answer.

_____

_____

_____

2. Is the scene between Mark and his mother typical of scenes in your house?   Yes ☐   No ☐

3. How would you describe Mark's behaviour?

        Passive ☐   Assertive ☐   Aggressive ☐

Give a reason for your answer.

_____

_____

_____

Sexual orientation

A person's sexual orientation basically describes whether someone is heterosexual, homosexual or bisexual. The majority of people are heterosexual, which means that they are attracted to people of the opposite sex to themselves. It is believed that up to 10 per cent of people are not heterosexual but are instead homosexual or bisexual. Being homosexual means that you are attracted to people of your own gender or sex. Female homosexuals are often called 'lesbians' and males called 'gays'. People who are bisexual are attracted to both males and females.

Not much is yet known about how our sexual preferences come about. Some people believe that we have no control over our sexual orientation, that we are born heterosexual or homosexual and cannot change the fact. Others believe that how our sexual orientation develops depends on our life experiences.

In the past, in Ireland, it was illegal to be involved in a homosexual relationship. Now it is illegal to discriminate against people because of their sexual orientation. However, it must be remembered that, just because the legal ban on homosexuality has been lifted, prejudice against the gay and lesbian community has not ended.

Homosexual acts are punishable by death in Sudan, Afghanistan, Pakistan, the Chechen Republic, Iran, Saudi Arabia, Mauritania, the United Arab Emirates and Yemen. Of these, three – Afghanistan, Iran and Saudi Arabia – are known to have executed homosexuals in the past 10 years.

Activity

The letter below has been submitted to a teenage magazine called *Attitude* by a young gay man. Read the letter, discuss it with your group and then, as a group or as individuals, write a suitable reply.

Dear Attitude,

I am sixteen and gay and I go to an all-boys secondary school. It's not as though being gay is something I chose, and it isn't something that I can change. The thing is I know my family will never accept me for who I am because they are so old-fashioned and they will think that it is disgusting and perverted. I feel really alone and unable to tell those nearest to me the truth. I did tell my best friend Paul the truth at the start of the year, but this has caused the death of our friendship. He became distant and we stopped hanging round together. He then proceeded to poison most of my friends against me and told all the other lads in school that I was gay and they bullied me to the point where I had to drop out of school. Six months ago I made a vain attempt at suicide trying to swallow as many pills as I could, but my stomach rejected them almost immediately. I made two more attempts and am growing used to damaging myself. The last time I tried my mother caught me. She doesn't understand what is going on and wants me to open up to her, but I am afraid that she will hate me. I know my father will throw me out of the house. I don't want to disappoint them and feel that I would be better off dead. Please help me.

Anonymous

Your reply:

_____

_____

_____

_____

_____

_____

_____

Below is a piece written by a lesbian woman in her twenties. Read the piece and then as a group look at and work through the discussion points that follow.

The hardest part about being a lesbian for me wasn't admitting it to myself, but building up the confidence to do something about it. Being young, alone and a lesbian can be both confusing and scary. When I told my friends they were taken aback at first but they then guided me and pushed me in the right direction. The first time a friend took me to a gay club, I was overwhelmed by the amount of people my own age who had come out. I felt that I had finally found people who understood how I was feeling and wanted to help me fit in. Some time after this I came out myself. When I came out to my parents, they were devastated. My mother couldn't stop crying and my father wouldn't speak to me. The thing was they did not understand what it was to be gay and assumed the worst. With time, they began to see how my friends and my work colleagues totally accepted my sexuality and I think that helped them a lot. It was a while before they told my extended family, meaning my aunts and uncles. When they finally did, they were surprised by the slight reaction they got. Now three years on I have a girlfriend who they accept and like. I think for them, like me, the worst part was pretending it wasn't there, and not talking about it. But with time and patience, they grew to see it as a natural and positive part of my life.

Discussion points

• Society's attitudes to homosexuality

• How are these attitudes shown by society, e.g. language used to describe homosexuals?

• Your own attitudes to homosexuality

• The difficulties you would experience in trying to keep your sexuality a secret

• The difficulties you would experience in 'coming out'

• Homosexuality as a positive thing, e.g. the high levels of creativity among homosexuals.

• Homosexuals as parents

Exam Time

Social Education (2003) – Long question (part)

1. Read this short report and answer the questions which follow.

Ω   **DAILY TIMES**   Ω

Vol. 37   Monday 20th January 2003

INCREASED DEMAND FOR MARRIAGE COUNSELLING

Report by: Sue Russell

The number of couples seeking counselling has increased dramatically in recent years. The majority of these couples have been married for less than six years.

'Time Poverty' emerged as the biggest problem facing many couples. Greater financial demands on couples means that many are working long hours in very stressful environments. Failure to communicate also ranked high on the list of marital problems. Other sources of difficulties included domestic violence, infidelity and alcohol abuse.

A. "'Time poverty' emerged as the biggest problem facing many couples." In your own words explain what is 'time poverty' means.

_____

_____

B. Counselling is a positive way of dealing with relationship difficulties. Explain whether you agree or disagree with this statement.

_____

_____

C. Explain **one** other positive method of dealing with conflict.

_____

_____

2. Look carefully at the cartoon. What do you think the cartoon is trying to tell us about relationships?

_____

_____

_____

_____

_____

3. Parents are responsible for the physical, social and mental well-being of their children. Under the following headings list **one** task involved in taking care of a three-year-old child.

Physical _____

Social _____

Mental _____

Unit 3 *Coping with Problems*

During this unit you will be looking at some of the more common problems or difficulties that people may meet in life. You will be finding out what agencies exist to help people to cope with these life crises. You will be required to use this information to complete the fourth and final key assignment of this module. The following are the problems that this unit will address, although you may like to investigate others which may be more important to you.

- Loss/bereavement
- Sexual harassment
- Addictions
- Mental illness
- Rape
- Sexual abuse
- Unexpected pregnancy

Loss/Bereavement

When someone close to you dies, this can seem like the biggest life crisis that someone can have to endure. This is because of the finality of death. Unlike other life crises, death cannot be fixed or put right; we can only cope and learn to live with our loss and grief.

Whether the death was sudden or expected, it is normal to experience a huge number of emotions and feelings such as disbelief, shock, anger, guilt, and sadness.

Disbelief

This is often the first reaction when someone close to you dies. The death seems like a nightmare, not real. This sense of disbelief can stay for a long time.

Shock

Shock is another common reaction. You may feel numb and stunned, and you may not be able to think clearly; everything is happening in a haze.

Longing and searching

Most people experience a sense of longing: to be able to speak or hear or hold the person one last time.

Anger

This is a normal response to death. People need to be able to be angry with someone for their loved one's death. They may be angry with God for letting them die, or with doctors or medical staff for not doing enough to save them. They may be angry with themselves or someone else for something they have done or not done. For example, if a child runs out in front of a car, the bereaved parents are likely to feel anger with the driver of the car.

Guilt

This is a very common reaction. People tend to go over events surrounding the death and blame themselves for not doing something more to prevent it. They may feel guilty about not having spent enough time with the person, or because they had arguments with them.

Despair, depression, loneliness and sadness

Very strong feelings of sadness and hopelessness frequently follow a death. You may lose interest in everything and even the smallest of tasks takes a lot of effort, for example you may sit round the house all day without even changing out of your night clothes. Other symptoms of despair and depression can be sleeplessness, loss of appetite, poor concentration and constant crying.

Physical reactions

When someone close to you dies, you may experience physical as well as emotional effects. Some common physical reactions are tiredness, headaches, sleeplessness, loss of appetite, pains in your muscles, pains or a tightness in your chest, nausea and diarrhoea.

Helping yourself through your grief

- Talk to others about how you are feeling.
- Don't cut yourself off from others.
- Give yourself time.
- Don't take comfort in drugs or alcohol; this is only masking over the feelings, not dealing with them.
- Get rest and exercise; try to eat well.
- Write about how you feel.

Helping others through their grief

- Do not avoid the subject of the person's death.
- Allow the person to talk about how they feel. Don't keep giving advice as usually the person just wants you to listen, not to find a solution to their problems.
- Help by doing practical tasks, e.g. tidying the house.
- Allow the bereaved person to cry, and don't be afraid to cry yourself.

Where to go for help

All of the eight health boards offer bereavement counselling. Below is a list of their main telephone numbers. If you ring these numbers. they will help you contact the service suited to your needs.

Dublin (north)	(01) 8823303	North-West	(071) 9852000
Dublin (south)	(01) 4632800	South-East	(056) 7761400
Mid-West	(061) 316655	South	(021) 4921641
Midlands	(0506) 46730	West	(091) 548321
North-East	(046) 9076400		

Sexual Harassment

Sexual harassment, in law, consists of deliberate and unwelcome sexual advances, unwanted requests for sexual favours, and certain other offensive conduct of a sexual nature. Sexual harassment may be committed by men or women in many different roles, such as that of boss, client, co-worker, fellow student, or teacher. However, a large majority of cases involve the harassment of women by their male bosses or fellow employees. Most countries have laws against sexual harassment.

The law recognises two types of employment-related sexual harassment: (a) quid pro quo and (b) hostile environment. Quid pro quo harassment occurs when a person in authority requires sexual favours from an employee in exchange for things, such as getting hired or promoted or not getting fired. Quid pro quo is a Latin phrase meaning one thing in return for another.

In hostile environment harassment, the offender does not demand an exchange. Instead, a pattern of behaviour makes the victim's job so unpleasant that their work is affected. The harassment may consist of asking sexual favours, making sexual comments, telling sexual jokes, or displaying pornographic pictures.

Sexual harassment is not confined to the workplace. People can be sexually harassed anywhere from pubs and clubs to walking down the street. The reason why a lot of the laws focus on sexual harassment in the workplace is that people's livelihoods or education can often be put at risk because of it.

Activity

1. What kind of behaviours do you think constitutes sexual harassment?

_____

_____

_____

2. What would you do if you found you were being sexually harassed in the workplace?

_____

_____

_____

Drug Addiction

In Module 1 we looked closely at some of the common drugs that are available in society today. We looked at the effects of taking these drugs. You should revise this section now. Addiction is one of the biggest and best recognised effect of drug taking and it is this aspect of drug taking that we will discuss now. Frequently drug addiction or more correctly 'drug dependence' occurs together with or after some life crisis. It then becomes a life crisis in itself. This is why we are looking at the problem now in this section of your course.

The World Health Organisation in 1964 described drug dependence as:

> 'A state, psychic and sometimes also physical, resulting from the interaction between a living organism and a drug, characterised by behavioural and other responses that always include a compulsion to take the drug on a continuous or periodic basis in order to experience its psychic effects, and sometimes to avoid the discomfort of its absence. Tolerance may or may not be present.'

Activity

Read the definition above a few times, then put it in your own words.

_____

_____

_____

_____

Physical dependence

Physical dependence occurs when the body adapts to repeated use of the drug. It is thought that some drugs actually replace our natural stress-defence mechanisms and therefore when the drug is taken away we have fewer stress-defence mechanisms than someone who never touched the drug, and can therefore suffer acute withdrawal symptoms.

Psychological dependence

Strong psychological or mental dependence is a characteristic of some drugs. This occurs because the user begins to associate the drug with mental well-being, with feeling calm and happy. The user then begins to think that they cannot have these feelings without the drug and so craves the drug and the feelings that it bring with it. This is psychological dependence.

Some drugs cause both physical and psychological dependence. These include:

- heroin
- alcohol
- barbiturates, e.g. sleeping tablets
- minor tranquillisers
- nicotine

Others are thought to have no physical dependence, although withdrawal symptoms can still be very strong. These drugs include:

- cocaine
- amphetamines, e.g. speed
- cannabis

Tolerance

With repeated drug use the individual needs more of the drug to achieve the same effects. A tolerance is built up and may be caused by two factors: the body becomes able to get rid of the drug more quickly, and the brain adapts to the drug, so that more of the drug is needed to get the same effect. A heroin addict can take 100mg or more of heroin in one injection. This dose would probably kill a non-addict.

Withdrawal symptoms

Withdrawal symptoms are experienced when a user stops taking some addictive drugs. The type of symptoms experienced depends on the drug. Sometimes withdrawal symptoms can be very severe as with heroin addiction where chills, pains and flu-like symptoms are often experienced.

Sometimes a drug substitute is given to make the withdrawal symptoms less severe. In the case of heroin, the most common drug substitute is methadone. At present there are 6,886 people waiting for methadone treatment. The only real cure for withdrawal symptoms is time, so that the body can begin to function as normal without the drug.

Where to get help

Usually when someone feels they have a drug or alcohol problem, they contact their GP or family doctor who will be able to refer them on to a suitable service in their area. There is a booklet called the Directory of Alcohol, Drugs and Related Services in the Republic of Ireland, available free from your local health promotion unit.

These are listed in Module 1, page 50. The telephone numbers of all the health boards are in the coloured pages of your local telephone directory under 'Department of Health and Children'. This will be a central number, but they will be able to put you in contact with the relevant service.

In addition there are a number of self-help organisations:

Alcoholics Anonymous
109 South Circular Rd, Dublin 8
Tel. (01) 4538998/4537677

Alateen (For teenage children affected by
a parent's drinking)
5 Chapel St., Dublin 1
Tel. (01) 8732699

AL-Anon
(For adult men and women affected by
someone else's drinking)
5 Chapel St, Dublin 1
Tel. (01) 8732699

Narcotics Anonymous
Tel: (01) 6728000 (Dublin)
     (021) 4278411 (Cork)

All of the above numbers are central numbers. They will be able to advise you on your local branch. These numbers are listed in the coloured pages of your local telephone directory under 'Personal Emergency Numbers'.

Mental Illness

Given that one in nine people in Ireland will suffer some form of mental illness and require treatment in a mental health unit at some time, this topic is a very important one. If these statistics are realistic, it seems likely that all of us will encounter mental illness during our lifetime either in ourselves, a family member or in a friend.

The cause and treatment of mental illness can be very complex and in some ways is not very well understood. This unit will not be focusing on the causes and treatments of mental illness but rather on allowing you to examine your own attitudes to mental illness and looking at how you can help maintain good mental health for yourself.

Often when we picture someone with mental illness we take the most extreme example as our guide. We picture someone who is very obviously ill, a person who cannot hold down a job, cannot form and keep relationships or even look after themselves properly. This is frequently a very inaccurate picture. Many people who are mentally ill do hold down jobs, do have families and generally live life and behave 'normally'. They may be able to cope with life in this way on the surface, while at the same time be struggling for happiness and self-fulfilment on the inside.

Activity

Attitudes to mental illness
Usually when we are prejudiced or ignorant about something or someone and have a negative attitude towards them, we make up hurtful names to describe that person or thing. People with mental illness are often described in this hurtful way.

Mental illness questionnaire

Tick whether you agree or disagree with the statements below. You may like to discuss your answers in groups afterwards.

	Agree	Disagree
1. Many mentally ill people are violent.	☐	☐
2. Most mentally ill people need to be kept in special hospitals.	☐	☐
3. Mentally ill people should be encouraged to live in the community.	☐	☐
4. Most mentally ill people are lost causes. They will never be right.	☐	☐
5. All mental illness is inherited, and so there is nothing you can do to stop it.	☐	☐
6. Mental handicap and mental illness are the same thing.	☐	☐
7. Asking for help means you are a weak person.	☐	☐
8. You cannot live a 'normal' life with a mental illness.	☐	☐

Promotion of mental health

Although some mental illnesses, e.g. schizophrenia, are thought to be largely genetic and their onset mainly beyond the control of the individual, others are thought to be more related to environment and lifestyle.

Physical well-being is thought to be very important for emotional or mental well-being. It makes sense, therefore, to eat a good diet, take plenty of exercise, not to smoke or use other harmful drugs and, if you drink, not to exceed healthy limits. If we look and feel healthy, our self-esteem is likely to be higher, which is an essential ingredient for mental health.

In addition to looking after ourselves physically, we need to look after our emotional side as well. It is important to have relationships that are close and trusting. We need someone with whom we can talk things over and share our feelings. If something is wrong or worrying us, we need to have someone that we can talk to without fear of them telling others or making fun of us.

All of us need a degree of routine and security in our lives. We need to know that we have somewhere safe to live where we will not feel threatened in any way. We need to feel part of a family or a community in order to feel valued and wanted.

All of us have a need for leisure time. It is best if we use this leisure time constructively by doing things we enjoy. Many people who spend too much of their lives working suffer mental illness. They literally burn out. This does not have to be someone who has a high-powered job; a lone parent who gets no time to him or herself may equally burn out.

Even if we do try our best to take good physical and emotional care of ourselves, there is no guarantee that we will not suffer from mental illness. The important thing is if you do become that one person in nine who suffers mental illness, you will not be ashamed or frightened to get help.

Activity

Read the case study below. What factors in Michael's life may put him at risk of mental illness?

Hi, my name is Michael and I am 21 years old. I left school at 16, the year after I did my Junior Cert. I am not in regular employment at the minute and don't really want it. The thoughts of going to the one place doing the same old thing every day would drive me mad. I prefer to do a bit of work here and there. Nothing too serious, just enough to get me money for going out. My favourite pub in the town is O'Briens. They know me well in there, as I go there most evenings for a few pints. You can smoke a bit of blow in there too and they don't seem to notice. If they do they do nothing about it which is sound. They serve grand pub grub. A bit greasy but it fills me up and stops me getting too drunk.

Last weekend I was in there from 3 o'clock. I met a girl. Don't ask me her name though. I can't really remember. I was a bit under the weather you see! I haven't had a steady girlfriend and don't want one, not since the last one. She really broke my heart and I swore never again. Love them and leave them is my attitude now.

I used to play football for the local team, the 'young Emmets'. I was pretty good. Last week I met Sean Purcell who manages the senior team. He was on at me to come back. I couldn't be bothered with that now. It would take too much effort to get fit again and they would be nagging me to give up the cigarettes. I can do without that hassle.

My mother is on at me to go on a diet. She's one to talk! Sometimes I get a bit depressed about my life and the way it has gone. The teachers at school used to tell my mother I had brains to burn if I'd only use them. If I get down in the mouth, I just go down to O'Briens and have a few drinks. That usually does the trick.

Factors that put Michael at risk of mental illness:

1. _____
2. _____
3. _____
4. _____
5. _____

Track 17

Listen to Track 17 and then answer the questions below.

1. Who was the first person to suspect that Joan was suffering from mental illness?

_____
_____

2. In what ways did Joan not fit the stereotypical image of a mentally ill person?

_____
_____
_____

3. What symptoms of mental illness did Joan have?

_____
_____
_____

4. How did Joan try to cope with or cover up these symptoms?

_____
_____
_____

5. What attitude did Joan's family have to her illness?

_____
_____
_____

6. Joan refers to Andy as a 'fair weather friend'. What do you think she means by this?

_____

_____

_____

7. How has Joan now learned to cope with her illness?

_____

_____

_____

8. In what ways, if any, did listening to Joan's story change your attitude to mental illness and mentally ill people?

_____

_____

_____

Rape

Rape is the name given to the crime of forcing sexual intercourse on a person against their will. Both men and women can be rape victims. The attacker may force the victim to submit to him by beating or threatening him or her with a weapon.

Victims do not ask to be raped. Statements like, 'she shouldn't have been out alone' or 'she shouldn't have been dressed like that', wrongly excuse and take responsibility away from the rapist. It must be remembered that the vast majority of men could see a thousand scantily dressed women walking alone in a remote area and never in a million years rape them.

Experts believe that rape together with marital violence are Ireland's most under-reported crimes. It is estimated that only one in four rapes are reported to the gardaí, and that of these reported rapes only a small percentage lead to an actual conviction.

Why are so few rapes reported?

• Most rapes are carried out by someone known to the victim. This prevents some victims reporting the crime.

• A medical examination is usually required within 24 hours of the rape. This can be very traumatic for the victim.

• Fear of publicity during the rape trial or of what the attacker will do when released from prison can put off many victims.

- Having to re-live the experience during the trial may be too traumatic for some victims.

Note

Unlike in some American states (as often portrayed in films) a woman's sexual history cannot be brought in as a defence in this country.

The rape victim's name and address cannot be made public.

Rape is a crime; it is the state not the victim that prosecutes the attacker. This means that the victim does not have to employ a solicitor or have legal costs.

Many women are taking self-defence classes to learn how to protect themselves.

If you are being attacked – although the attacker may have a weapon
- Shout as loudly as you can for help.
- Hit out or push the attacker away.
- Kick the attacker in the shins.
- Spray perfume or deodorant in the attacker's eyes if you have these in your bag.
- Run to a public place or a house.

Common feelings after a rape attack
- Numb
- Angry
- Depressed
- Afraid
- Contaminated
- Helpless
- Guilty

What you should do
- Do not keep it to yourself; tell someone.
- Report the attack to the gardai.
- If you need to go to the doctor do not go alone; bring someone you trust with you for support.
- Talk to someone in a Rape Crisis Centre. They will know best how to support you.

Man Found Guilty of Rape

An unemployed docker was found guilty today of raping his former girlfriend at an apartment once occupied by both of them in the city centre. The rape was said to be all the more harrowing as it was committed in the presence of their 3-year-old daughter. Paul Owens (29), who claims that he has been having severe bouts of depression since he split up with the victim, was remanded in custody to Mountjoy Jail where he awaits sentencing on Monday.

1. Do you think it matters that the victim was once Paul Owen's girlfriend? Explain your answer.

2. Why do you think that Paul Owen raped this young woman?

3. What should the woman do now to help herself and her child?

Rape Crisis Services and Centres in Ireland

Dublin	70 Lower Leeson St., Dublin 2.	(01) 6614911
Cork	5 Camden Place, Cork.	(021) 4505577
Galway	7 Claddagh Quay, Galway.	(091) 589495
Limerick	11 Upper Mallow St., Limerick.	(061) 311511
Clonmel	14 Mary's St., Clonmel, Co. Tipperary	(052) 27622
Waterford	2A Waterside, Waterford.	(051) 873362

Activity

Look through local and national newspapers for reported rape cases. Discuss them in class. Take special note of the following issues:

1. Many people think rape is a crime committed by strangers. Do the articles that you have read bear this out?

2. What kind of sentences do the rapists receive in the cases you have read?

3. Is there anything else that you notice or think is important to point out after reading the articles?

Points to discuss:

• Can sex offenders be rehabilitated?

• Do you think that convicted sex offenders should be tracked by gardaí after finishing their prison sentence?

Unexpected Pregnancy

Shock, numbness and fear are the words often used by young women who are faced with an unexpected pregnancy. To many women who have not yet completed their education or secured a fulfilling job, unexpected pregnancy can create a great deal of pain, indecision and confusion. Many feel totally alone. Perhaps they are not in a very secure relationship and do not know how the baby's father will take it. Others fear the reaction of family, neighbours and friends. Some young women who have had an unexpected pregnancy report how they kept their pregnancy to themselves for long periods of time, putting off dealing with the fact for as long as possible.

Where to go for help and advice

The Irish Family Planning Association

Head Office: Solomons House, 42a Pearce St., Dublin 2. Tel: (01) 4740944.

This organisation provides the following services to women:
- Free pregnancy test
- Free pregnancy counselling
- Information and practical advice on all the options
- Continuing with the pregnancy and keeping the baby
- Adoption and fostering
- Abortion - information about clinics in England
- Pre- and post-abortion counselling

Telephone (01) 4740944 and they will advise on the address and phone number of the clinic nearest you.

CURA and LIFE

Both these organisations offer the following services:
- Free pregnancy test
- Counselling
- Practical and emotional support during and after the birth of your baby
- Referral to adoption and fostering agencies if requested.

Both these organisations do not consider abortion an acceptable option in any circumstances and will therefore not provide abortion information. They do, however, offer post-abortion counselling.

CURA

30 South Anne St, Dublin 2
Tel: (01) 6710598 or 1850 622626

LIFE

29 Dame St, Dublin 2
Tel: (01) 6798989 or 1850 281281

Both of the contact numbers above are central. If you ring them, they will be able to tell you the address and telephone number of the CURA or LIFE centre nearest you.

Abortion and the law

Abortion is currently not legal in Ireland under any circumstances. However, Irish women have the right to travel to England where abortion is legal during the first 24 weeks of pregnancy if the mother's physical or mental health is at risk. They are also entitled to information on abortion. Pre- and post-abortion counselling is advised.

Activity

Read Tom's story below and then answer the questions that follow.

I had just left college and this was my first job. The money and the prospects of promotion were good so I felt that I had really landed on my feet. Lorraine came to work in the firm on a college work placement, I fancied her the minute I saw her. After a few days I asked her to come for a drink with me after work and she did. We had a great time and talked and talked. We really seemed to have a lot in common. We continued to see each other even after she returned to college. Everything seemed perfect, our sex life was great and we really seemed to be made for each other.

Lorraine did not want to go on the pill so we used condoms as a method of contraception. On a few occasions we got bit careless about using them. Looking back it was really irresponsible of both of us.

Lorraine told me that she was pregnant on 12 January. That date will stick in my mind for the rest of my life. She was really upset about the fact. I don't really blame her, as she was a good bit younger than me and, unlike me, had not yet finished college. From the outset my gut reaction was to keep the baby, but Lorraine didn't want to. I offered to support her and the baby financially, and told her that she could always take time out and return to college later.

Lorraine comes from a very strict family and she really feared what they would say. In the end Lorraine decided that she was going to go to England for an abortion. She felt that she was too young to have a baby. I tried to persuade her not to but she said that it was her body and her life and that she had made up her mind. I was devastated. I even rang a solicitor to see what my rights were. I was horrified but not really surprised that I had really no rights.

Lorraine went to England on her own on 25 March and had the abortion the next day. I suppose I should have gone to support her but I could not bring myself to do so. I felt that what she was doing was wrong. When she came back, we were like strangers. She felt that I had let her down, and I felt that she had let me down. Things were never the same after that and we split up about three weeks later. That was four years ago. Even now I often wonder what might have been. What our baby would have looked like?

1. Why do you think Lorraine decided to have an abortion?

_____

_____

_____

2. How do you think Lorraine would have felt when she went to England?

_____

_____

_____

3. Do you think Tom should have gone with her? Explain your
answer.

_____

_____

_____

4. Do you think that fathers should have more rights? Explain
your answer.

_____

_____

_____

Child Sexual Abuse

What is meant by sexual abuse?

Child sexual abuse is a very difficult subject to approach in a classroom situation as it is
likely that someone in the class has experienced it in some form. Child sexual abuse is
when an adult uses his or her power or authority over a child to force or persuade him
or her to take part in sexual activities. Sexual abuse ranges from fondling or petting to full
vaginal or anal intercourse. Incest is when the sexual abuse is committed by a family
member.

Who sexually abuses?

Although both men and women sexually abuse, the majority of abusers are male.
Contrary to popular myth, most sexual abuse is committed by someone known to the
child - a family member, a neighbour, someone in authority or a baby-sitter. The sexual
offender can often appear to be very ordinary and have the trust of the child and of those
that care for him or her. This is very far from the truth. Child sexual abusers are very
disturbed, cruel individuals. They frequently know exactly what they are doing and go to
great lengths to cover it up. They are not usually psychiatrically ill. Sex offenders come
from all types of backgrounds. Some have very responsible jobs and are considered
upstanding members of the community. This is why in the past many child victims of
sexual abuse were not believed when they reported how they were being treated.

Who is abused?

Children from all types of backgrounds, both rich and poor, are abused. It is estimated
that in Ireland as many as one in eight girls and one in twelve boys are sexually abused at
some time before they reach their sixteenth birthday. There is no reported difference
between the numbers of children from urban or rural backgrounds being abused.

The effects of abuse

Sexual abuse affects different children in different ways, so although some general effects will be given here each child is unique, and how this terrible experience effects them will be different for each child:

- Loss of trust in all adults
- Poor self-esteem
- Extreme nervousness or panic attacks
- Feelings of guilt, as some children convince themselves that they are in some way responsible for what has happened to them
- Shame.

As the child moves into adulthood, they may have difficulty forming lasting sexual relationships. Because of low self-esteem they may get into abusive relationships, believing themselves to be undeserving of anything better. A person who has been abused as a child may go to sexual extremes, either being unable to have any sexual relationships or behaving very promiscuously. In an attempt to forget what has happened they may resort to alcohol or other drugs. However, with skilled help, victims of child sexual abuse can move on to a new satisfying life.

What help is available for victims of sexual abuse?

If you have been sexually abused yourself, or know someone who has been sexually abused in the past, there are organisations that can try to help. It is important to remember that because someone has been sexually abused does not mean that they will automatically develop permanent emotional problems.

The Dublin Rape Crisis Centre provides help for both male and female adults who have been sexually abused as children. Their address and phone number are:

Dublin Rape Crisis Centre
70 Lower Leeson St
Dublin 2
Tel. (01) 6614911
Freefone 1800 778888

Key Assignment

For this key assignment you should write out on a sheet of paper a list the agencies or organisations that help with health or addiction problems. List the address and phone number and state what services they provide.

Some of the agencies you might like to include are: Irish Family Planning Association, Alcoholics Anonymous, CURA, Rape Crisis Centre, Childline, LIFE, Narcotics Anonymous, Aware, Al-Anon, Al-Teen, the Samaritans. Keep this key assignment in your Social Education folder as evidence of completion.

When you have completed this key assignment, go to the beginning of this module and tick it off on the checklist.

Module 5

Contemporary Issues 2

This module should be completed during session 3 (Year 2).

Below are seven key assignments for this module. You should choose FOUR of these. One of them must be a group activity and one must be an out-of-school activity. As you work through the module and do your chosen assignments, come back to this page and tick off each of them.

1. I took part in a debate on a contemporary issue.

Date: _____

2. I examined a contemporary issue with a group of students in my class. Then each one of us presented this issue in a different format: as a short report, press release, news broadcast, image, article for a school magazine, collage or illustrated fact sheet.

Date: _____

3. I wrote to my local newspaper or political representative about an issue of interest to me.

or

I presented an illustrated fact sheet about a contemporary issue.

Date: _____

4. I tracked an issue in a newspaper or on television for three days and gave a brief report to my class about it.

or

I created a two-minute slot for a radio programme in support of a local issue.

Date: _____

5. I gave a brief report to my class about crime in my local area.

Date: _____

6. I took part with others in a roleplay about my civil rights.

Date: _____

7. I collected a registration form, filled it in and posted it off to register my name on the List of Electors.

Date: _____

Unit 1 *Influences on Contemporary Issues: The Media*

In this unit you will be looking at various contemporary issues in terms of how different factors, such as media sensationalism and bias, can affect our thoughts and opinions about these issues.

Activity

Media Survey

1. Which of these media forms would be generally available to you at home?

TV	☐	Radio	☐	CDs/tapes	☐
Video	☐	Internet	☐	Magazines	☐
Newspapers	☐	Journals	☐		

2. Which of the above would you use most?

1._____   2._____   3._____

3. Have you watched the news in the past week?

Yes ☐   No ☐

4. Have you read a newspaper in the past week?

Yes ☐   No ☐

If yes which one? _____

5. Do you watch documentaries regularly?   Yes ☐   No ☐

If yes, what was the last one you watched? _____

6. Do you use the internet regularly?   Yes ☐   No ☐

If yes, what do you generally use it for? _____

Young People and Contemporary Issues

Activity

Some issues are of more concern to young people than others. In your group brainstorm for as many of these issues as possible. From this list pick the eight most popular ones among your group. Record these below.

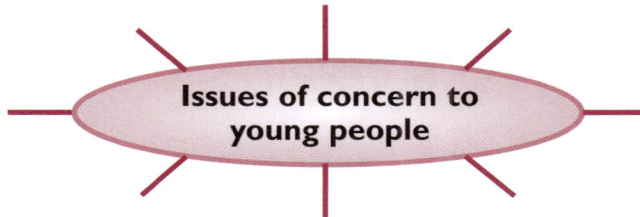

Issues of concern to young people

As a group, over a period of time gather local and national newspapers. Try to have a mixture of both tabloid (e.g. *The Star*) and broad sheet (e.g. *The Independent*) newspapers. Examine the newspapers for each of the issues recorded above. Cut out all of the relevant articles and display them. As a group reads through them, paying particular attention to the following points:

• How many of the issues were reported on?

• Were the issues dealt with in detail?

• Were photographs or captions included?

• Were the issues given an important place in the papers, e.g. at the front?

• What was the paper's tone/attitude to the issues?

• How were young people portrayed in the articles?

Key Assignment

For this key assignment your class must divide up into groups of approximately six students. Each group should pick a contemporary issue of interest to them. These issues must be examined in detail, with each group member then reporting on the issue using a different format: as a short report, press release, news broadcast, image, article for a school magazine, a collage or an illustrated fact sheet.

When you have completed this key assignment, go to the beginning of this module and tick it off on the checklist.

Example: Press release

Date: ⟶ *This is the date you send the press release to the paper.*

Embargo: ⟶ *You are telling the paper not to publish the details of the release until this date; if there is no embargo you write 'none'.*

Contact: ⟶ *Name of person sending the press release to the paper.*

Give your press release a clear heading

Huge Shopping Complex to Put Small Businesses in Jeopardy

Navan Chamber of Commerce warned today that if the proposed mega shopping complex on the Dublin road were to go ahead that it would spell disaster for small businesses in the town.

Those in favour of the complex claimed that it would pose no threat to existing traders. Councillor James Ryan, who is in favour of the complex, claimed that, 'because the population of Navan is growing so rapidly there is enough business for everyone'.

Local traders are planning a protest march to the county council offices on Friday next.

Ends

Press releases need to be precise and to the point giving all the relevant details. Type up using double spacing. Write 'ends' so that the editor knows the article is finished. You can include quotes from people involved in the issue.

Example: News broadcast

The person who chooses this format will have to come up with a story and then write out a script for it. They will then have to tape record themselves delivering the broadcast. Listen to the sample news broadcast on Track 18 and answer the questions.

1. Why is the Catholic church described as a 'burden' in this article?

_____

_____

_____

2. What did the minister say about anti-AIDS funding?

_____

_____

_____

3. What is your opinion of the Catholic Church's opposition to contraception?

_____

_____

_____

How Events Become Issues

Sometimes one particular event, because it gets publicity, can trigger a debate and in this way become an issue. Take the following examples. Write down what issues these events raise.

Three young boys lose their lives when 14-year-old David Hawks opens fire on his classmates in a New York high school.

Issue(s) _____

_____

A well-known Dublin solicitor is given four years for the killing of Laura Jones in a drunken driving accident, two years ago. Laura's family is horrified by the light sentence.

Issue(s) _____

_____

Twelve-year-old boy is driven to suicide by classmates' cruelty.

Issue(s) _____
_____

The mother of four-year-old Suzanne Roe, who weights almost six stone, fears that her daughter could die without urgent medical attention.

Issue(s) _____
_____

Track 19

Listen to the debate on Track 19, and then answer the questions.

1. What is the motion for this debate?

_____

2. What are the main points put forward for the motion?

_____
_____
_____

3. What are the main points put forward against the motion?

_____
_____
_____
_____

4. How did both speakers try to make the debate more interesting?

_____
_____
_____
_____

5. If you were debating this issue, would you be for or against the motion? Explain your answer.

For ☐   Against ☐

Reason _____
_____
_____

Key Assignment

For this key assignment you must take part in a debate about a contemporary issue.

When you have completed this key assignment, go to the beginning of this module and tick it off on the checklist.

Possible motions

Irish people should be very sympathetic to the cause of the refugee.

There is no excuse for the unemployed.

A student's life is an easy one.

Cannabis should not be made legal.

Divorce is not a good idea.

Drugs should be allowed in sport.

Add some motions of your own.

_____

_____

_____

Contemporary Issues and the Media

Usually the way we learn of contemporary issues is through the media. Generally it is only issues very local to us, for example issues concerning people in our parish or our town that we learn about first hand. The media, therefore, has a very big influence on how various issues are presented and on how public opinion is formed. Sensationalism and bias are two characteristics of the media that can sometimes distort or colour our understanding of various contemporary issues.

Activity

Look up the words 'sensationalism' and 'bias' in a dictionary and write down what you find below.

Sensationalism

_____
_____

Bias

_____
_____

Law and Disorder

Last night there was a confrontation in Wexford town as gardaí sought, in highly charged circumstances, to prevent more Travellers joining the group of 400 already illegally parked on land owned by the Department of the Marine. Local publicans have closed their doors and the hotel opposite the Travellers did so as well.

Prior to this incident, it might have been argued that local businesses were over-reacting. Publicans had been saying they were forced to close their premises following a number of incidents involving Travellers. The gardaí said no such incidents were reported to them.

No doubt groups representing Travellers would say many of the publicans were inspired out of pure prejudice to close their doors. But businessmen will rarely do such a thing without good reason.

In any case, whatever doubt there was about the action of the publicans has been erased by the intransigence displayed last night.

This may now force the hand of the gardai. They had been saying that although they had the legal authority to move on this group, they lacked the manpower to do so. Apparently up to 200 gardaí and 30 tow-vans would be needed to move the 100 caravans. It is hard to believe such a force could not be mustered if the will was there. If it wasn't there before, it should be now. A group of this size cannot be allowed to illegally occupy land and cause such disruption.

The law can only have a deterrent effect if it is enforced, and if the only way to enforce it on this occasion in Wexford is to call in more gardaí, then this is what must be done.

No society can function unless each group respects the rights of others. This rule has to apply both to the majority of the community and to minorities. Sometimes we are tempted to think that the majority has all the duties and the minorities all the rights. This is a two-way process.

**Irish Independent
4 June 2004**

Activity

1. Why do you think this large group of Travellers may have gathered together in Wexford on this occasion?

2. Do you think there would be the same reaction if a large group of settled people camped here on this Department of the Marine site for, say, a rock concert of motor bike rally? Explain your answer.

3. Local publicans have closed their doors. The article says 'Prior to this incident, it might have been argued that local businesses were over-reacting' – does the article explain what it is that the Travellers have done? Is it clear from the article what 'this incident' is?

4. The article states that 'no such incidents were reported to' gardaí. Please comment on this.

5. Whose opinions are represented in this article?

6. In your opinion is this a fair and balanced article or is there evidence of bias? Explain your answer,

7. How do you think you would feel if you were one of the Travellers in this situation?

_____

_____

8. Comment on the headline given to this article.

_____

_____

Key Assignment

For this key assignment you are required to track or follow an issue on TV or in the newspapers for three days. You must then report to the class about the issue.

When you have completed this key assignment, go to the beginning of this module and tick it off on the checklist.

Issue tracking

What issue are you tracking?

_____

Are you tracking the issue through the papers?   Yes ☐   No ☐

If so, which paper(s) are you using?

_____

Are you tracking the issue through the news?   Yes ☐   No ☐

If so, which station are you looking at/listening to?

_____

Day 1
Date _____

What were the main points made by the broadcast/article?

_____

_____

_____
_____
_____
_____

Day 2

Date _____

What were the main points made by the broadcast/article?

_____
_____
_____
_____
_____
_____

Day 3

Date _____

What were the main points made by the broadcast/article?

_____
_____
_____
_____
_____
_____

Track 20

Listen to Track 20. On it an LCA student interviews a member of a local action group about a local issue. This interview is an example of a two-minute radio programme slot. Answer the questions that follow.

1. What issue is being addressed in the interview?

_____
_____

2. What action group does Cathy represent?

_____
_____

3. What are the main concerns of this action group?

_____

_____

_____

4. What information do they base their concerns on?

_____

_____

_____

5. What is Cathy's group doing to help the issue?

_____

_____

_____

Key Assignment

For this key assignment you are required to create a two-minute slot for a radio programme in support of a local issue.

When you have completed this key assignment, go to the beginning of this module and tick it off on the checklist.

Exam Time

Social Education (2003) – Long question (part)
1. Name a contemporary issue you have studied. Name and explain how you could use **one** type of media to help in a campaign approach to that issue.

_____

_____

_____

2. What action did you take or could you have taken, to help this issue?

_____

_____

_____

Unit 2 *Influences on Contemporary Issues: Interest Groups*

Interest groups exist for one of two reasons:
- To promote the interests of their members, e.g. Irish Farmers Association.
- To promote a cause which is usually for the common good, e.g. Greenpeace works for the preservation of the earth's environment.

When an interest group tries to make changes at government level around an issue of importance, the interest group sometimes becomes called a 'pressure group'. Pressure groups try to make changes in some or all of the following ways:

Lobbying	Putting pressure on politicians.
Campaigning	Getting public interest by organising different events, advertising campaigns, etc.
Awareness raising	Putting together information programmes and leaflets.
Non-violent action	Marches, protests, strikes, boycotts.

The main aims of these actions are usually one and sometimes all of the following:

- To improve a service.
- To change government policy.
- To change attitudes/behaviour of the public.
- To protect human rights.
- To prevent a disaster.

1. What message is this poster trying to get across?

_____

_____

_____

_____

_____

2. Do you think that this poster is effective?

Yes ☐ No ☐

Explain your answer.

_____

_____

_____

_____

_____

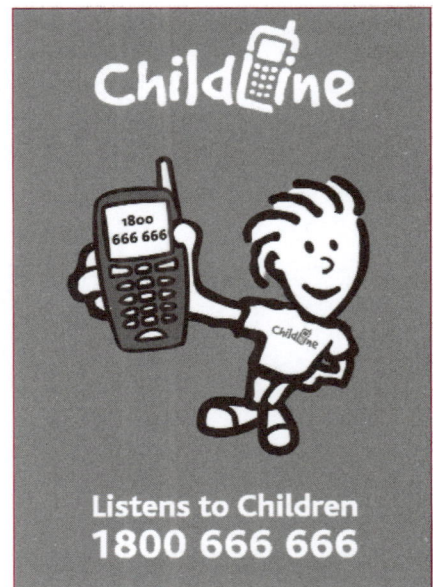

ChildLine

1800 666 666

Listens to Children
1800 666 666

Key Assignment

For this key assignment you must:

A. Write a letter to your local newspaper or political representative about an issue of importance to you.

or

B. Present an illustrated fact sheet about an issue of importance to you.

Keep a copy of your letter/fact sheet in your Social Education folder as evidence of assignment completion.

When you have completed this key assignment, go to the beginning of this module and tick it off on the checklist.

Key Assignment

For this key assignment you must give a brief report to your class about crime in your area. Below are some ideas as to where you can get information for your report.

When you have completed this key assignment, go to the beginning of this module and tick it off on the checklist.

Read articles in your local newspaper

Talk to a neighbourhood watch representative

Interview an elderly person about how they feel

Crime in my area

Give your own experiences

Talk to the local gardaí

Listen to local radio

Below is a list of interest groups, find out (perhaps you could phone them):

A. What the main aim(s) of each of the groups are.

B. What contemporary issue(s) is each group concerned about.

C. How they try to make changes concerning the issue(s) of importance to them.

Find out the same information about one or two local interest groups campaigning in your area. Keep the information you find out in your Social Education folder. It may be of use when you do your contemporary issue task.

Interest groups

ISPCC	Pavee Point
ISPCA	ICA
Trocaire	IFA
Amnesty International	INOU (unemployed)
Greenpeace	Irish Wheelchair Association
Focus Ireland	Irish Refugee Council
Oxfam	National Youth Council of Ireland
Barnardo's	

Land Mines Horror Is Girls' School Subject

Students at Our Lady's College, Greenhills, Drogheda, recently had the opportunity to explore and learn of the devastating effects of land mines when they participated in 'one world week' organised by the Development Education for Youth (under the National Youth Council). The aim of the week is raising awareness about global peace, justice and development issues. This year's theme was 'young people imagine'. The local students were engaged in considering the land mines issue from various angles, focusing particularly on the horrific way in which innocent lives are destroyed or seriously endangered by land mines.

In a war situation, they were told that armies plant anti-tank and anti-personnel mines, the latter of which are very inexpensive weapons to produce and that continue to kill and maim long after hostilities have ended. A single mine can cost up to $1000 to remove.

At present 64 countries are contaminated by between 80-100 million mines. Every month, over 2000 people are killed or seriously injured. Apart from those already planted, another 100 million mines remain stockpiled.

They will continue to inflict pain and suffering on the innocent men, women and children of such countries as Afghanistan, Cambodia, Angola, and Mozambique for many years to come.

It should not be forgotten that the mines do not come from the countries that they destroy, but from Italy, France, Germany, Britain, China, America and the former USSR.

In countries plagued by land mines, daily tasks such as collecting water or firewood or walking in the paddy fields can have deadly consequences.

A child who sets out for school in the morning will be mutilated if he or she bends down to pick the butterfly-shaped objects. From an economic point of view, food-producing land, a precious resource in developing countries, is rendered useless when any number of mines are detected. This important point was emphasised in the Greenhills exhibition which featured an actual land mines 'warning sign', brought from Cambodia by Garda Andrew Tuite – who was part of the UN team there to supervise elections.

Ireland is one of only seven signatories to the inhumane weapons convention calling for a land mines ban. Speaking in Geneva in July this year the minister for state and foreign affairs stated that, 'the Irish Government are totally opposed to the manufacture, stockpiling, transfer, export, sale and use of land mines'. As a matter of policy Ireland does not manufacture or trade in any form of land mines. We will play our part in convincing other governments that a total ban on mines is the desirable objective.'

Statements like this must be encouraging to a group such as Pax Christi, which is working for peace and justice in the world.

The general secretary of its Irish section, Mr Tony d'Costa, visited Greenhills to show slides to the students and to share his knowledge on the experiences of mines in Cambodia, Angola, Afghanistan and Iraqi Kurdistan.

The students saw images of mines in various types of terrain, people who had lost limbs in an explosion, and deminers at work in the field.

Mr d'Costa was accompanied by Dr Pierre Ryckmans, a Belgian landmines expert, who has called on members of the Oireachtas foreign affairs committee to lobby the other member states of the EU to take a position on the land mines issue.

Until 1989, Belgium, a member of NATO, had been a land mines producer but as a result of public pressure, the Belgian Parliament became the first in the world to ban the production, transfer and use of land mines.

Dr Ryckmans spoke to the girls about his work with mine victims in Angola. He is now involved in the International Landmines Campaign of Handicap International, an organisation that treats mine victims and helps to rehabilitate them.

The Greenhill's students had a unique opportunity to see close up the casings of anti-personnel land mines which had to be demined. The students were shocked that such small 'harmless' looking objects could cause such dreadful carnage.

Drogheda Independent

Activity

1. Can you name three countries that are infested with land mines?

_____

_____

2. Why do you think so many land mines remain unremoved in these countries?

_____

_____

3. Name three countries that make land mines.

_____

_____

4. Why do you think these countries continue to make land mines?

_____

_____

5. Land mines cause economic problems for the countries infested by them. Explain this statement.

_____

_____

_____

6. What does the organisation Pax Christi aim to achieve?

_____

_____

7. Name one method or strategy used by Pax Christi to achieve this aim?

_____

_____

9. What does Dr Pierre Ryckmans want the Irish Oireachtas to do?

_____

_____

10. What does the organisation Handicap International do in relation to the land mines issue?

_____

_____

South Africa: How Dunnes Stores workers made a difference

In July 1984 a group of eleven Dunnes Stores workers were suspended without pay from their jobs. The reason for this was that the workers were refusing to handle goods manufactured in South Africa, which practised apartheid laws. The workers mounted a picket outside the Dublin shop where they worked and stayed on strike for the next two and a half years. In 1985, partly due to the publicity created by the Dunnes workers, the Irish Government announced its proposal to restrict all imports of South African fruit and vegetables. The eleven Dunnes Stores workers made a difference. They met Nelson

Mandela when he visited here in 1990. He praised them for standing up for the human rights of non-whites in South Africa.

Exam Time

Social Education (2004) – Short questions

1. Which of the following is a voluntary organisation that assists the needy in your area?

Amnesty International ☐

Dept. of Social and Family Affairs ☐

St. Vincent de Paul ☐

2. Select **three** of the organisations below and briefly explain what each does.

1. _____

_____

2. _____

_____

3. _____

_____

Unit 3 *Democratic Institutions*

Local Government

Local government, sometimes called the local authority, takes care of the day-to-day business of your local area. The local authority is under the supervision of the Ministry for the Environment and is made up of two parts:

- Elected members
- Full-time manager

Depending on where you live your local authority will have a different name. Your local authority may be called any one of the following:

- Borough council
- Town commission
- County borough council
- Urban district council
- County council

How local authorities are elected

Local elections are held usually every five years. Every person who is 18 years of age or older on 15 April in the year of the elections and living in the area is entitled to a vote. You do not have to be an Irish citizen to vote in local elections. People who want to be elected onto the local authority must nominate themselves or be nominated by someone else and declare themselves up for election. On voting day, the public come and cast their votes, the votes are counted and local authority members for the next 5 years are declared elected.

Each local authority elects a chairperson or leader who chairs local authority meetings, etc. In Dublin and Cork the chairperson of the local authority is called the Lord Mayor. In areas with a county council (rural areas) the chair is called a chairman or chairwoman. In county boroughs and borough councils (large towns) a mayor is elected.

Who are your local authority members?

Activity

It is important to know the names of the people in your local area who have been elected as local authority members and therefore represent you. Your local authority members are called councillors or in the case of smaller towns – town commissioners. Find out who your local councillors or town commissioners are and write their names below.

_____   _____
_____   _____
_____   _____

Activity

For this activity you must find out the functions of your local authority. These functions can be put broadly under eight different headings. Look at all the jobs or duties listed in the box below and place them under whichever of the eight headings you think is the most appropriate one. When you have finished discuss each of the functions, and think about how well your local authority is carrying out its duties.

Public toilets   Pest control   Litter wardens   Land drainage

Local authority mortgages   Managing housing list   Traveller halt sites

Driving licences   Tourism development   Management of industrial sites

Theatres   Urban renewal   Sewage schemes

Public library   Providing local authority housing   Homeless provision

Maintaining local authority houses and estates   Bin collection

Repair of existing roads   Car registration   Art galleries   Museums

Public swimming pools   Parks   College grants   Traffic wardens

New roads/motorways   Planning permission   Road signs

School attendance officers   School traffic wardens   Car tax

Helping VECs (schools)   Maintenance of graveyards   Tip head maintenance

Preparing for elections   Maintenance of courthouse   Rate collection

Public water supply   Public recreation centres   Flower beds

Air pollution control   Water pollution control   Fire brigade

Housing/building

Road transport and safety

Water supply and sewage

Development incentives and controls

Environmental protection

Recreation and amenities

Agriculture, education, health and welfare	Miscellaneous

National Government

Activity

Ireland is a democracy. Find out what this means and write your findings below.

I think a democracy is:

_____
_____
_____

The dictionary says a democracy is:

_____
_____
_____

The Oireachtas is the name given to the Irish parliament or National Government. The Oireachtas is made up of three different parts; these are:

- The President
- The Dáil
- The Seanad

An Taoiseach's Office

The Constitution

The Constitution of Ireland (Bunreacht na hÉireann) is a document that lays down the laws of this country. Members of the Oireachtas, like the general public, must abide by the laws laid down in the constitution. The laws contained in the constitution cannot be changed without holding what is called a referendum. During a referendum the people of the country vote to either change some law in the constitution or to leave it as it is. Every Irish citizen over the age of 18 and entered onto the register of electors can vote in a referendum.

Sample Referendum paper

Brief instructions on the correct manner of voting
The title of the bill proposed to amend the Constitution
Yes ☐   No ☐
The voter marks x in either the Yes or No box

List of Recent Referenda	Year	List of Recent Referenda	Year
Joining EC	1972	Divorce	1995
Voting age	1972	Bail	1996
Recognition of specified religions	1972	Cabinet confidentiality	1997
Adoption	1979	The Amsterdam Treaty	1998
University representation in the Seanad	1979	Northern Ireland Peace Treaty	1998
		Local government	1999
Right to life of the unborn	1983	Death penalty	2001
Voting right at Dáil	1984	International Criminal Court	2001
Single European Act	1987	The Nice Treaty	2001
Right to travel	1992	Abortion	2002
Right to information	1992	Citizenship	2004

Activity

Pick an issue and hold your own referendum in class. Use the sample referendum paper above as a guide.

As already stated, the Oireachtas or Irish parliament is made up of three parts – The President, the Dáil and the Seanad. Each of these will now be looked at in turn.

The President

The office of President is the highest in the land. Presidential elections are held every seven years (unless a President dies in office) and a President can serve for two terms, which would be a total of 14 years. In order to stand in a presidential election you must be at least 35 years old. Every citizen of Ireland over the age of 18 is entitled to vote in presidential elections.

The role of the President

The main role that the President has in this country concerns issues related to the constitution. In recent times, though, the office of President has become a very public one and the President often represents Ireland abroad.

Past presidents of Ireland

Douglas Hyde	1938-1945
Sean T O'Kelly	1945-1959
Eamon de Valera	1959-1973
Erskine Childers	1973-1974
Cearbhall O'Dalaigh	1974-1976
Patrick Hillery	1976-1990
Mary Robinson	1990-1997
Mary Mc Aleese	1997-

Others since this book was printed

_____   _____

_____   _____

The Dáil – TDs

In total there are 166 seats in the Dáil. After an election these seats are filled by TDs, or Teachta Dála, from all over the country. From these 166 people the Government, or cabinet, is picked.

The Government

The Government consists of between 7 and 15 people. Within these numbers there must be:

- The Taoiseach (Prime Minister)
- The Tánaiste (Deputy Prime Minister)
- The Minister for Finance

There are also a number of other ministers who take particular responsibility for various government departments. Government ministers are also called cabinet members.

Activity

Who is the current Taoiseach? _____

Who is the current Tánaiste? _____

Below is a list of government ministers. Find out who is the minister currently in each of the positions.

Minister for Enterprise, Trade and Employment

_____

Minister for Marine and Natural Resources

_____

Minister for Public Enterprise

_____

Minister for Foreign Affairs

_____

Minister for Agriculture and Food

_____

Minister for Finance

_____

Minister for Heath and Children

_____

Minister for the Environment and Local Government

_____

Minister for Social Community and Family Affairs

_____

Minister for Arts, Heritage, Gaeltacht and the Islands

_____

Minister for Defence

_____

Minister for Justice, Equality and Law Reform

_____

Minister for Tourism, Sport and Recreation

_____

Minister for Education and Science

_____

Someone in your class could ring Leinster House's public relations office to get this information – Tel. (01) 6183066/ 3166, Fax (01) 6184118.

The Seanad

The Seanad consists of 60 senators and it also sits in Leinster House. The main function of the Seanad is to advise the Dáil.

European Representation

Ireland joined the European Community (EC) in 1973. Other countries have joined since then and the EC continues to grow with new countries applying to join every year. The idea behind the EC is that there is strength in numbers. This means both economic strength and military strength. There are three main institutions or bodies that make up the European Community or Union. These are as follows:
- The European Parliament
- The European Commission
- The European Council

The European Parliament

The European Parliament has 732 members (called MEPs), of whom 15 are from Ireland. European elections are held every five years. The European Parliament is much like the government of any country. It has various departments that deal with the day-to-day running of the European Community.

Name an MEP that has been elected to the European Parliament from your constituency or a constituency near you:

_____

Who is the current President of the EU? _____

The European Commission

The European Commission mainly concerns itself with the EU budget and making sure that members of the EU uphold the laws of the union.

Ireland has one European Commissioner. Can you name him or her?

_____

The European Council

Ministers from all the member states, together with heads of national governments (the Taoiseach in our case), meet to discuss various issues concerning the EU and its member states. Which ministers are called to the council depends on the nature of the matter that has arisen, for example, the movement of beef throughout the EU would concern our Minister for Agriculture and Food and she or he would go along to represent Ireland's views at the council meeting.

Activity

1. What is the Constitution?

_____

_____

2. The Oireachtas or the Irish Parliament is made up of three parts. Can you name them?

_____

_____

_____

3. What political parties are currently in government?

_____

_____

4. Name our current Taoiseach. _____

5. How many TDs sit in Dáil Éireann at any one time?

_____

6. What are independent TDs?

_____

7. What is meant by the opposition party?

_____

8. In what way is Europe becoming like one big country?

_____
_____
_____

Exam Time

Social Education (2002) – Short questions
1. The head of the Irish government is known as the:
Taoiseach ☐   President ☐   Ceann Comhairle ☐

Social Education (2003) – Short questions
2. Local Authorities are under the supervision of which minister?
Minister for the Environment ☐
Minister for Finance ☐
Minister for Education and Science ☐

3. Which of the following was **not** a President of Ireland?
Mary Robinson ☐
Douglas Hyde ☐
Charles Haughey ☐

4. In what year did Ireland join the EU?
1963 ☐   1973 ☐   1983 ☐

Unit 4 *Active Citizenship: Voting/The Budget*

Elections

There are five different kinds of elections in this country. These are as follows:

Local elections — These are elections to the local authorities and elections occur usually every five years. Elected people are called county councillors or town commissioners.

By-elections — This is when a TD dies or resigns and his or her seat becomes vacant. An election is then held in his or her constituency to fill the vacant seat.

General elections — These are national elections held to elect the Dáil, and occur at least once every five years.

Presidential elections — These are held every seven years to elect the President (unless the President decides to stay for a second term and nobody else comes forward).

European elections — These are held every five years to elect people to represent us in Europe (MEPs).

In addition to these five elections people are also asked to vote in referenda. Referenda occur when there is a proposal to change the Constitution.

Register of electors

This is a list of all the people registered to vote in elections. A new Register of Electors is compiled and published by the local authority each year. New people are added to it including those who have reached the age of 18, and people who have legally come to live in this country.

Anyone can look at the register. It can be inspected at any of the following locations:

- Local authority offices
- The county registrar's office
- Public libraries
- Post offices
- Garda stations

Key Assignment

For this key assignment you must register to vote. To do this you should collect a registration form from your local post office or county council/corporation office. Fill in the form as you approach your eighteenth birthday and then post the form to the Registrar of Elections at your county council or corporation office. The address will be in the government services section at the front of the phone book.

When you have completed this key assignment, go to the beginning of this module and tick it off on the checklist.

Activity

Have your own class election. This will help you see how a real election works.

A simulated election

1. Compile the register of electors.
To do this you will have to list the full name, address and age of everyone in your class. This list will be your Register of Electors. Put a number beside each person's name.

2. Fill in polling cards.
Some time before an election a polling card is posted to each person named on the Register of Electors. On the day of the election voters should bring this polling card together with a form of identification to their polling station. Fill this sample one out below.

Polling information card

Your name and address

_____

_____

_____

Your number on the Register of Electors _____

The name of your polling station

_____

---

3. Compile a list of candidates and design a sample ballot paper.

Below is a list of five candidates on a sample ballot paper. In this election imagine there are three seats to be filled. This means that three candidates will be elected and two will not. The question is which three? Notice that the candidates are listed in alphabetical order. Before this ballot paper would be considered a valid one, it would have to be franked or stamped at the polling station. On the ballot paper you mark your first preference 1, your second 2 and so on.

Track 21

Before you vote, listen to each of the candidates telling you what their views are and what they would do if elected. (Please note that the 'politicians', parties and party policies depicted are all fictitious.)

Mark order of preferences in spaces below.	
	BURNS (Conservative Party) NEIL BURNS, of 18 Conor Avenue, Ringsend, Dublin 4, (GP)
	CAROLAN (Environmental Party) SARAH CAROLAN, of 64 Little Wood, Glasnevin, Dublin 9, (Pharmacist)
	NUGENT (Liberal Party) SEAN NUGENT, of 23 Park St., Dublin 1. (Company director)
	RYAN ALAN (Social Democratic Party) ALAN RYAN, of 9 Ulster Avenue, Drumchondra, Dublin 9, (Teacher)
	SMITH HANNAH (Workers Party) HANNAH SMITH, of 23 Lake View, Swords, Co. Dublin, (Trade union leader)

(This page may be photocopied and used in your simulated election.)

4. Set up a simulated polling station, complete with a presiding officer (who oversees voting), a personation agent (who tries to prevent electoral offences, e.g. voting in someone else's name) and a secret ballot box to put the ballot papers in.

5. Everyone in your class votes and places the ballot paper in the box. Do this without letting anyone else see who you voted for. This is called voting by secret ballot and means that you can vote for whoever you like and no-one can put you under any pressure to vote one way or another.

Counting votes

In Ireland the system of counting votes is more complex than in some other countries, for example Britain where you vote for only one person and do not give second preference and third preference votes, etc. The system that operates in Ireland is called 'proportional representation'. It is basically as follows:

1. Spoiled or invalid votes are removed.
2. First preference votes are counted for each candidate.
3. A quota is calculated and if a candidate gets more votes than this quota in first preferences they are deemed elected.

How the quota is calculated

The quota is calculated by dividing the number of valid ballot papers (total poll minus spoiled votes) by one more than the number of seats in the constituency and adding one to the result. For example, in your election there are 28 people voting and there are three seats to be filled. The quota would be calculated thus:

$$\left(\frac{28}{3+1}\right) + 1 = 8$$

4. The elected candidate's extra votes are divided up among the other candidates according to what the second preference is on these. If there is no second preference indicated on the papers, they are put aside.

5. Counting goes on like this until all the seats are filled.

In the case of the presidential elections there is only one seat to be filled, that of the office of President. In this case the first person to reach the quota becomes President. The returning officer declares the results of the election.

What three candidates did your class elect?

Name of candidate

_____

_____

_____

Activity

Have an election to find out what the three most popular Leaving Certificate Applied subjects are. Put 1 beside your favourite subject, 2 beside your next favourite and so on.

Mark order of preferences in spaces below.

	ARTS EDUCATION (Art, drama, music, dance, etc.)
	ENGLISH AND COMMUNICATIONS
	GAEILGE
	INFORMATION TECHNOLOGY
	LEISURE AND RECREATION
	MATHS APPLICATIONS
	MODERN LANGUAGES (French, German, Spanish, etc.)
	SOCIAL EDUCATION
	SPECIALISM (1) _____
	SPECIALISM (2) _____
	VOCATIONAL PREPARATION AND GUIDANCE

Which three turned out most popular?

_____

_____

_____

A politician's clinic

For elections to the Dáil the country is divided up into 41 different areas or constituencies. Each constituency or area elects a number of TDs.

Which constituency do you live in?

_____

Because a TD is elected by the people of a certain constituency, he or she is there to represent them and to work on their behalf. TDs keep in touch with their constituents by holding what are called politician's clinics. People can come along to these clinics and raise their issues and concerns with the local politician. The politician then tries to give help and advice. Depending on the nature of the problem, the TD may contact ministers, government departments, the council or corporation, health board or any other state body to help solve the person's problem.

Activity

What are the names of your local TDs?

_____
_____
_____

When and where do they hold their clinics? (This information is available in local newspapers or from Dáil Éireann.)

_____
_____
_____

What kind of issues do you think people bring to advice clinics?

_____
_____
_____

Legislation

Perhaps the most important function of the Oireachtas (President, Dáil and Seanad) is to 'enact legislation'. This means making new laws and changing old laws that are outdated.

All legislation begins as a bill, which is a proposal for a law. If the bill is accepted at all it goes to the Dáil where it is debated by the TDs. Amendments may be made to it resulting from these debates.

If the bill is passed by the Dáil it goes to the Seanad and they look at it. The Seanad cannot prevent a bill from going through; it can only delay it. When they pass the bill, it goes to the President.

The President then looks at the bill and checks that it does not go against the Constitution. The President can decline or refuse to sign the bill, or on the other hand if the President is happy with the bill he or she signs it into law. It is then sent to the Supreme Court so that it will be adopted into law.

Activity

Find out what bill(s) are going through the Oireachtas at the minute. You may have to ring Leinster House's public relations office on (01) 6183066/3166 to find this out or visit their website: www.irlgov.ie/oireachtas

---

The Budget

Once a year, in December, the Minister for Finance presents the budget to the Dáil. The national budget is like a family's budget in that it is an attempt to balance the country's spending with its income. The budget lays out how much and in what ways the Government is going to raise its income for the year. The minister will outline proposals for new taxes and changes to the existing taxation system.

The budget also sets out how the state will spend its income. The budget estimates how much is to be spent on the gardaí, army, schools, hospitals, social welfare payments, housing, etc. After the minister presents his budget, it is debated in the Dáil. Sometimes if there is big opposition to parts of the budget, changes may be made before it comes come into action in the following April.

Activity

Examine the budget in December. The evening news, budget summaries in the newspapers, current affairs programmes will all provide you with the information you need. Write down three budget proposals.

_____

_____

_____

_____

Note: Information on all recent budgets is available on
www.budget.gov.ie (click I'm feeling lucky button, if you are using
the Google search engine).

Activity

Imagine you are the Minister for Finance preparing the budget.
You have a limited amount of money to spend. List three things
you think would spend money on.

1. _____
2. _____
3. _____

Exam Time

Social Education (2002) – Short questions

1. To vote in a general election in the Republic of Ireland,
a person must be an Irish citizen.

                                             True ☐   False ☐

2. A general election in the Republic of Ireland must take place
at least once every:

        2 years ☐   5 years ☐   10 years ☐

Social education (2004) – Short questions

3. A referendum is held in Ireland to:

    Change the constitution ☐   Elect the President ☐

                                             Pass the budget ☐

4. From the word-bank, select the term which is correct for each
of the following.

A. A vote taken to change Bunreacht na Éireann (the Irish
Constitution) is called a _____.

B. The name given to a member of a local authority is

_____.

C. A person who sits in the European Parliament is called an

_____.

D. Government of the people by the people is called

_____.

Local election	Referendum	General election
Polling station	President	Councillor
MEP	Chairperson	Spoiled vote
Quota	Democracy	

Social Education (2003) – Long question (part)

5. These are the main political parties in the Republic of Ireland. Select **three** different political parties and name a TD from each party.

Political Party	TD
1.	
2.	
3.	

Unit 5 *Civil Rights and Responsibilities*

Understanding the Law

The law in Ireland can be broadly classified under four different headings:

Statute law

This branch of the law contains what are called acts. As detailed in the previous section, bills become acts if they are passed by the Dáil, the Seanad and the President. An example of an act is the Intoxicating Liquor Act 1988. This act prohibits the sale of alcohol to anyone under the age of 18, and the buying of alcohol for someone under 18.

Case law

When a case comes to the High or Supreme Court, the judge makes a decision on it based on similar cases which have occurred in the past.

Constitutional law

The Constitution of this country was drawn up in 1937. It is a list of rights, responsibilities and social principles. An example of a right would be the right to a fair trial, a responsibility would be to respect your neighbour, a social principle would be that the state promises to support the institution of the family.

Common law

Common laws have been followed for many years, but have not been formally written down like constitutional laws.

Some legal terms explained

Degree of intent	If you are arrested and charged with a crime, how your crime will be judged will depend a lot on whether you intended to commit the crime or not.
An indictable offence	A serious offence, usually with trial by jury.
A summary offence	A more minor offence, usually tried in the district court.
Larceny	Stealing.
Robbery	Stealing but using force or fear to do so, e.g. mugging.
Burglary	Stealing from a house or vehicle.

(If any of these offences are aggravated, this means that the criminal had a weapon.)

To be put on remand	This is when the judge does not pass sentence there and then, but will do so at a later date or else pass the case on to a higher court. People can either be remanded in custody (locked up) or remanded on conditional release with or without bail.
Bail	This is a sum of money paid to the courts by a friend or relation of a person accused of a crime. If the person does not turn up in court the next time, the bail money is lost.
The DPP (Director of Public Prosecutions)	This office looks at the book of evidence against an individual accused of a crime and decides whether there is enough evidence to go ahead and prosecute. If the office of the DPP thinks there is, they will prosecute on behalf of the people of Ireland.
In camera	All family law cases such as applications for barring orders, legal separations, etc. are held in camera, which means in private. The general public cannot attend.

The Courts

(See the illustration on the next page.)

Understanding Your Rights and Responsibilities

- A member of the gardaí can stop and search you in the street if they think you are in possession of an illegal drug.

- If you are arrested, you must give the gardaí your correct name and address.

- If you are driving a car, motorbike or other vehicle, a guard can stop you, ask you to give your correct name and address, and to produce your licence and insurance within 10 days. You must also allow yourself to be breathalysed.

- If you are under 18 years of age, you must have a parent or other responsible adult there with you while being questioned by the gardaí.

- If you are over 14 years of age, it is assumed that you know right from wrong.

- You have the right to talk to a solicitor.

- If there is a warrant for your arrest, the reason for your arrest will be written on it. You have the right to see this document.

The Irish Court System

Supreme Court
Highest court in the land.
Five judges.
Decisions made by this court must be followed in the future by lower courts.

High Court
Hears criminal and civil cases (when hearing criminal cases called the Central Criminal Court) and appeals from lower courts.
Sometimes a jury.
Decisions made by this court must be followed in the future by lower courts.

Court of Criminal Appeal
Hears appeals from other courts.

Special Criminal Court
Three judges, no jury.
Deals with terrorist type offences.

Central Criminal Court
Really the High Court when it is hearing criminal cases.
Judge and jury.
Hears serious criminal cases.

Circuit Court
Sometimes has a jury. Sometimes cases are sent here by the District Court judge. This court also hears appeals against District Court decisions.

Children's Court
Deals with cases involving under-18s.
There is a separate children's court in Smithfield, Dublin. Outside Dublin, however, the children's court is held at a special sitting of the District Court. The media or the public are not allowed into the Children's Court. The media cannot identify a young person appearing in this court.

District Court
Local court. More minor offences, no jury, usually a fine is imposed instead of a sentence. Deals with barring orders, maintenance payments, etc. All family law is held 'in camera', which means in private. The maximum sentence for an offence is 12 months, although this can go up to 24 months if you are being tried for more than one offence.

Under the Education Welfare Act you must remain in full-time education until you have reached the age of 17, or 16 if you have a Junior Certificate or FETAC qualification. You should not without good reason (certified illness) miss any more than 20 days in any one school year.

The juvenile diversion scheme

This scheme was established in the 1960s to prevent young offenders going to court and getting convictions that would stay with them for the rest of their lives. To qualify for this scheme, usually you must:

- be under 18;
- not have been in serious trouble before (although sometimes second and third time offenders are still allowed to avail of the scheme);
- admit to your crime.

Also, your parent or guardian must agree to you being put on the scheme, and sometimes the victim of your crime must also agree.

You will be registered with the National Juvenile Office in Dublin.

If you have committed a crime and are accepted under this scheme you will be given either an informal or a formal caution. (Formal is given at the station; informal usually in your own home.)

From here you will be referred to your local juvenile liaison officer (JLO). The job of a JLO is to help you to keep out of trouble. They will encourage you to join clubs and get an education. He or she will supervise you in this way for two years or until you are 18 years old, whichever comes sooner.

If you for some reason are not accepted under this scheme (for example your crime is serious or you are a frequent offender) you will have to go to court. If you are under 16, you will be tried in private in the District Court or in the Children's Court in Smithfield. It is very rare for juveniles to be tried by jury.

If you are found guilty, the judge may ask for a report on you before he or she sentences you. A probation officer will make out this report. Such reports investigate your background, health, whether you have drug or alcohol problems, etc.

The judge may dismiss the charge, fine you, fine your parent(s), order you to do community service, instruct you to meet with your probation officer on a regular basis, send you to a residential home or a detention centre. It is rare and very unsatisfactory for a juvenile to be sent to prison.

Activity

Answer true or false to the following statements:

	True	False
Stealing a bicycle is an indictable offence.	☐	☐
'In camera' means that TV cameras are permitted in the courtroom.	☐	☐
If arrested, you can legally remain totally silent.	☐	☐
Larceny means deliberately burning down someone's building.	☐	☐
Aggravated assault means assault with a weapon.	☐	☐
JLOs supervise young offenders for up to two years.	☐	☐
Murder, rape and such crimes are tried in the District Court	☐	☐
Decisions in the Supreme and High Court have implications for the lower courts.	☐	☐
There are occasions when you can be searched without a warrant.	☐	☐

Key Assignment

For this key assignment you are required to take part with others in a roleplay about your civil rights. Below are some suggestions; you should try some of your own as well. It may be necessary to invite a local garda or JLO in to talk to your group and advise you about your civil rights before doing your roleplay.

You are walking along the street drinking out of a can of cider. You have a bag with three or more cans in it. A garda stops you.

A squad car pulls up at your house. They believe that you have in your possession some stolen CDs.

You have been arrested for shoplifting and you are now in the police station. You have the stolen goods on you.

You are refused entry to a shop in town.

You are a passenger in a stolen car. The gardaí catch up with you and arrest you, the two other passengers and the driver.

Around the World

Capital punishment

Capital punishment is punishment by death for committing a crime. Since the early 1800s, most executions have been because of murder convictions. The death penalty has also been imposed for such serious crimes as kidnapping, armed robbery, rape, and treason.

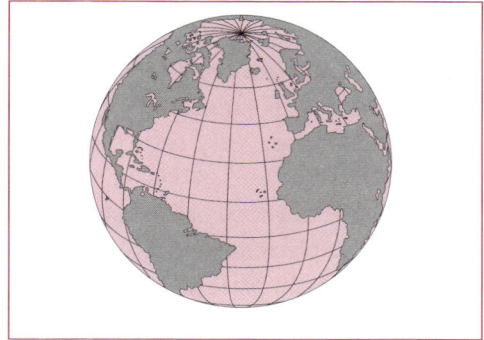

People disagree about whether capital punishment is moral or indeed effective against crime. Many people oppose the death penalty, chiefly because they consider it cruel. Critics also warn against the risk of executing innocent people by mistake. Supporters of capital punishment believe that, in some cases, people who take human life deserve to lose their own lives. Many supporters believe that the threat of death discourages crime more than the threat of prison. However some studies have shown that there is no big increase in murders when the death penalty is abolished in a country or state.

In the past 25 years, approximately 430 people have been executed in America. As many as 3,500 people are or have been on death row over this period. The method of execution varies from state to state. Three states – Delaware, New Hampshire and Washington – still permit hanging. Eighteen states still permit death by firing squad. Other common methods include the gas chamber, electrocution and, most common of all, death by lethal injection.

Lethal injection

A fast-acting barbiturate (sedative) is first injected to put the prisoner to sleep. Two additional drugs are then injected to stop the prisoner's breathing and heartbeat. Death usually occurs within minutes after the injections. The first execution by lethal injection occurred in Texas in 1982.

Some people believe that lethal injection is more humane than other means of execution, such as the electric chair and the gas chamber. Opponents of the death penalty, however, argue that any method of execution is inhumane. Most condemned prisoners who have had a choice between lethal injection and other methods of execution have chosen the injection.

What is your opinion?

Kangaroo courts

Kangaroo court is a slang term for a group of people who take the law into their own hands, by acting as judge and jury. Such groups usually disregard the principles of law and justice, and impose very severe punishments.

The term is thought to have arisen in Kansas or Ohio in the United States. Judges travelled from place to place holding trials quickly, and were paid with the fines of convicted prisoners. This hopping from place to place gave rise to the term 'kangaroo court'.

In Northern Ireland, loyalist and republican paramilitaries such as the UVF and the IRA operate 'kangaroo courts'. People who commit crimes such as drug dealing, joyriding or robbery are punished, usually by kneecapping. In the case of more serious crimes the person may be threatened with death if they do not leave the country.

What is your opinion?

Vigilante groups

Vigilante groups are self-appointed citizens groups who illegally fight criminal activity in their communities. Vigilante groups often form where people believe that regular law enforcement is inadequate. In the beginning these groups consisted of law-abiding citizens who formed anti-crime patrols and neighbourhood watch groups. Members notified the police of suspicious activity in their neighbourhoods. With the growth of drug abuse and other crime in the US and elsewhere a new type of illegal vigilante group was formed. In some cases vigilante groups have used arson and murder to rid their neighbourhoods of illegal drug dealers and other alleged criminals.

What is your opinion?

Islamic law

Countries such as Iran, Oman, Saudi Arabia, Libya, Northern Nigeria and Afghanistan have what is called Islamic law. Islamic law is a feature of Muslim countries and is based in their holy book which is called the Koran.

Under Islamic law the penalty for stealing is having your hand cut off. For other offences people are publicly flogged or stoned. In Iran over a hundred offences carry the death penalty. Public beheadings are permitted under Islamic law in Saudi Arabia.

What is your opinion?

Family law in other cultures

In most countries, one man marries one woman, and they stay married unless one of them dies or they get divorced. This system of marriage is called monogamy. Some societies permit a man to have more than one wife, or a woman to have more than one husband. The marriage of a man to more than one woman is called polygamy. Islamic law permits a man to have as many as four wives. A small number of societies practise polyandry, whereby a woman gets married to more than one man. This is the case among some Tibetan groups living in Northern Nepal. Among these people, a woman marries two or more brothers. The children of this family regard the oldest husband as their father, regardless of whether he is or not, and the other brothers as their uncles.

What is your opinion?

Exam Time

Social Education (2002) – Short questions
1. The maximum sentence for an offence in a District Court is:
          12 months ☐   18 months ☐   24 months ☐

Social Education (2003) – Short questions
2. What is punishment by death called?
          Capital punishment ☐   Corporal punishment ☐

Social Education (2003) – Long question (part)
3. Ireland has eight law courts. Name any **two** and explain how they work.

1. Name _____

_____

_____

2. Name _____

_____

_____

Unit 6 *Contemporary Issue Task*

This task should be completed during Session 3, in Year 2. For this task you are asked to investigate a contemporary issue of importance to you. Tasks may be undertaken as a group, but if they are your own individual contribution (what you actually did on your own) this must be made very clear to the examiner. Unlike some others, this task has three parts. If one or more parts are left out, marks will be lost. The three parts are:

1. Written task report: where you write about how you investigated your contemporary issue and what you found out.	2. Action: here you must carry out an action designed to (1) inform people about your issue and/or (2) do something to help or improve your issue.	3. Oral presentation: at the beginning of your interview you must make a short speech of 2-4 minutes about the issue you have chosen.

The Task Report

Your task report will have to contain sections on each of the following. This list may be useful as a table of contents.

1. Statement of aims
2. Planning
3. Research
4. Carrying out of action
5. Summary and analysis of findings
6. Evaluation and self-evaluation
7. Appendix

Stage 1 Deciding what to do?

This goes into your planning section.

Activity

As a group, brainstorm for interesting contemporary issues. The list of issues on pages 113-114 may help you. Record what you come up with on the next page.

Contemporary Issue Task Ideas

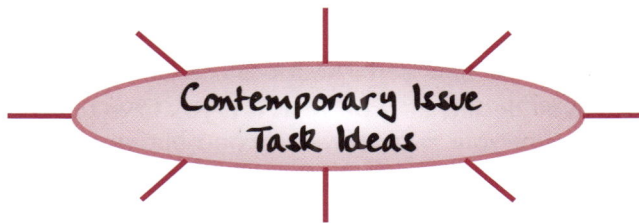

From this list pick the issue that you feel interests you most. Note: You may have to research a few issues before you can make this decision.

I chose _____ as my contemporary issue because

_____

_____

_____

Stage 2 Write out your list of aims

What do you hope to achieve by doing this task?

If yours is a group task, you must record group and individual aims.

Sample list of aims – issue: Travellers

Aims
- I aim to find out more about the issues and problems facing Travellers in Ireland today e.g. health, housing, education and discrimination.
- I aim to interview a Traveller from my area about their life and what being a Traveller means to them.
- I aim to find out more about Travellers in other countries, e.g. Roma, and make comparisons with Irish Travellers.
- I aim to find out more about Traveller interest groups.
- I aim to make a presentation to my classmates so that they will be better informed about the Traveller issue.
- I aim to carry out this task in an organised way so that I am happy with the work I have done and am finished on time.

Stage 3 Planning: what are you going to do and when are you going to do it?

This task should take a total of 10 hours to complete. This is not very long, so it is important that you decide early on what it is you have to do and make a plan for carrying work out.

Essential jobs

1. Research: Two types of research have to be undertaken for this task.
   - Primary research e.g. interviews, surveys, questionnaires.
   - Secondary research getting information from the internet, from newspapers or books.
2. You must look at your issue from at least two of the following perspectives:
   - local
   - national
   - global.

   In the Traveller example, the issue is examined from all three perspectives.
3. You must read all the research material that you gather and summarise and analyse your findings. There is no sense in having chunks of material from the internet or from books if you have not read it and showed you have understood it.
4. You must think of and carry out an action relating to your issue.
5. You must prepare a short (2-4 minutes) speech about your chosen issue for the examiner.
6. You must first evaluate how well you achieved your aims (task evaluation) and carry out a self-evaluation.

Activity

Record a first draft of your 10-hour plan below. Your real plan may not look like this, but this plan will help you think about what jobs need to be done first, second and so on. Your finished plan goes into the planning section of your task report.

Day 1 (1 hour) _____

_____

Day 2 (1 hour) _____

_____

Day 3 (1 hour) _____

_____

Day 4 (1 hour) _____

_____

Day 5 (1 hour) _____

_____

Day 6 (1 hour) _____

_____

Day 7 (1 hour) _____

_____

Day 8 (1 hour _____

_____

Day 9 (1 hour) _____

_____

Day 10 (1 hour) _____

_____

This is your planning section complete.

Stage 4 Research

As stated before, you must carry out two different types of research for this project – primary and secondary. Issues must be examined from at least two perspectives – local, national and global.

Carry out your piece of primary research in accordance with the guidelines for conducting research outline in Module 2 My Community.

Read all your secondary research material thoroughly. If you have internet printouts or photocopies from books or newspapers, use a highlighting marker to highlight important or relevant pieces of information. This indicates to the examiner that you have read the material. A common fault of students in this task is that they present the examiner with wads of unread secondary research material.

Stage 5 Presenting your findings

Present the findings from your primary research. Summarise the findings (main points) from your secondary research. Think about the following questions:

- Who is affected by the issue? How are they affected?
- What, if anything, is being done about this issue? Has there been any progress?
- What, in your opinion, could be done to help this issue?
- Has anyone something to gain from this issue remaining unresolved?

Stage 6 Prepare for and carry out action

The action you undertake must inform people about your issue and/or do something to help or improve your issue. Some actions that could be undertaken are:

- Put together a teacher's pack on your issue for CSPE students.
- Prepare a talk on your issue (perhaps with Powerpoint or overheads) and give it to your own class or perhaps to another class in the school.
- Write an article for your school magazine or even a local or national paper about your issue (see the example below).
- Organise a fund-raising event related to your issue.
- Make suggestions for the schools policy on the issue e.g. bullying, drugs.

This is an example of an action undertaken by a primary school in Co. Louth to tackle the issue of inactive children and traffic congestion.

First 'Walking Bus' Is Launched

The first 'walking bus' to be introduced in the North East was launched by Laytown N.S. on Tuesday morning when two groups of eager children clad in reflective jackets could be seen walking to school. The walking bus is a novel idea where volunteers who are usually parents act as 'bus drivers' and 'conductors' and collect children from pick-up points or 'bus stops' and walk them safely to school.

First piloted in England, the walking bus initiative was devised in a bid to promote a more active lifestyle for children, while at the same time reducing traffic congestion at schools.

Parents and children are very enthusiastic about the scheme and 40 volunteers have come forward and about 90 children are interested in travelling on the bus

**Drogheda Leader
2 June 2004**

Stage 7 Carry out evaluation and self-evaluation

While carrying out the evaluation and self-evaluation, it may help to answer the following questions.

- Look back at your aims, which of them do you think you achieved?

- How do you know that you achieved them?
- During the task generally what things do you think went well?
- What things did you find difficult or did not go so well?
- If you were to do this task again, which changes do you think you would make?
- Did you learn anything about yourself while doing this task?
- What skills did you develop or improve on while doing this task?
- What did you enjoy about doing this task?

Stage 8 Oral presentation about your task

You must make a short speech (2-4 minutes) about your task. You can use aids such as speaking notes, charts, display boards, video clips, photographs or a Powerpoint presentation.

Track 22

Listen to the young person on Track 22 making her oral presentation about Traveller rights. Answer the questions that follow.

1. What issue did this student choose to investigate?

_____

2. What did she do for her primary research?

_____

_____

3. Where did she get information for her secondary research?

_____

_____

4. What aid did she use to help her during this oral presentation?

_____

5. Would you give this student good marks for her oral presentation? Explain why.

Yes ☐   No ☐

Why? _____

_____

_____

Module 6

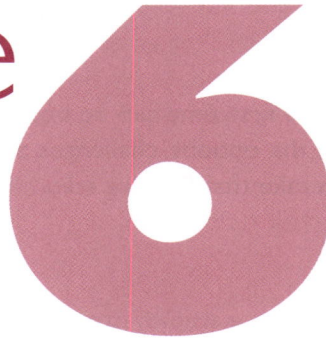

Taking Charge

This module should be completed during session 4 (Year 2).

Below are the four key assignments for Module 6. You must do ALL of these. As you work through this module and complete each one, come back to this page and tick it off.

1. I prepared a step-by-step guide to leaving home and finding a place to live. I included the different considerations that need to be taken into account.

   Date: _____

2. I conducted and recorded (either on tape or written) an interview with a young person living away from home.

   Date: _____

3. I prepared a weekly budget for a young person living on his or her own. I based this budget on the current weekly wage of a young person who has just started working.

   Date: _____

4. As part of a group, I participated in a discussion with a visitor representing a bank, credit union or building society, and reported on what I learned from the discussion.

   Date: _____

Unit 1 *A Place of My Own*

Moving out of home for the first time can be both an exciting and daunting time. In this unit we will be looking at the options, challenges and problems that a young person may face when they decide to take that first big step.

Key Assignment

Prepare a step-by-step guide to leaving home and finding a place to live. Include the different considerations that need to be taken into account. Complete the activities and listening exercises in this unit to fulfil the requirements of this key assignment.

When you have completed this key assignment, go to the beginning of this module and tick it off on the checklist.

Reasons for Moving Out

It is important that when young people decide to move out of home it is for a good reason and not because they feel that they have to, even though they do not want to or are not really ready to. This can lead to a disaster and much hardship and unhappiness for everyone involved.

Activity

Look at the list below of some of the more common reasons given for moving out of home. Tick whether you think the reason given is a good one or a bad one. Good reasons usually mean that the person has thought about what he or she is doing. Bad reasons tend to be the result of snap or emotional decisions.

	Good reason	Bad reason
To get away from nagging parents	☐	☐
To be able to come and go as I please	☐	☐
To be independent	☐	☐
To have a wild time drinking and going out	☐	☐
So my boy/girlfriend can sleep with me	☐	☐
To be near work/college	☐	☐
To get away from a violent or abusive home	☐	☐
To prove that I don't need anybody	☐	☐

Where To Live

When a young person decides to move out of home and find a place to live, money is usually the biggest factor that needs consideration when deciding on the type of accommodation most suitable. Even though you may pay some money to your parent(s) for your keep, it is usually only when you move out that the real cost of living becomes apparent to most people.

Here is a list of the usual accommodation types available for renting. Look at each of them and then decide which of them would be (a) the most expensive and (b) the most suitable for a person moving out of home for the first time on a limited budget.

A purpose-built flat or apartment
Digs
A self-contained flat within a large house
A flat within a large house with some shared facilities
A bedroom in a house with all other facilities shared
A bedsit

1. Which of these options would be the most expensive?

_____

2. Which of these options would be the most suitable for a young person moving out of home for the first time?

_____

Give a reason for your answer: _____

_____

Cost, while usually the biggest factor in deciding on where to live, is not the only factor. Put a tick beside the factors below that would be important to you.

Having my own bedroom ☐
Not having to share a bathroom ☐
Not having to share kitchen/sitting room ☐
Being in a good state of repair ☐
Having a washing machine ☐
Having central heating ☐
Having a telephone ☐
Having digital TV ☐

Being near shops, pubs, etc. ☐
Being near work/college ☐
Being tastefully decorated ☐
Having a garden ☐

Threshold is an organisation that provides information for tenants and landlords. Nominate someone in your class to write to or telephone Threshold. Ask them for two of their leaflets, *Renting for the First Time* and *Renting a Home from a Private Landlord*. You can also ask them for a sample rent book. You may have to pay a small amount for this.

Dublin	21 Stoneybatter, Dublin 7	(01) 6786096
Cork	8 Father Matthew Quay	(021) 4271250
Galway	Augustine House, St Augustine Street	(091) 563080

Read both these leaflets in class and underline the important points.

Finding a Place to Rent

If you are looking for a place to rent, you could try each of the following options:

- The 'to let' sections of local or evening papers, e.g. *Evening Herald*.
- Ads in shop windows around the area you want to rent in.
- 'To let' signs on the actual buildings.
- If you are a student, 'to let' signs on the college notice board.
- Word of mouth.
- Estate and letting agents.

Look at the classified advertisement and answer the questions that follow.

ADJ O' Connell St., D1, Gresham Hse., 1 bed, 2nd flr, own pkg space, F/F, G.F.C.H., p.tv, wash/dryer, profs only. €900pm, min 1 year.
Ph: (086) 7679543.

What do you think these abbreviations from the ad mean?

Own pkg space _____   F/F _____

p.tv _____   min 1 year _____

G.F.C.H _____   profs only _____

Activity

Look up three places to let in your local area. A small number from your class might want to visit an estate agent or look through a copy of your local paper and telephone to find out the following information about the accommodation.

Address	Rent	Deposit due	Facilities
1.			
2.			
3.			

Viewing accommodation

Track 23

Fiona and Catherine are viewing a flat. Listen to the conversation they have with the landlord and then the one they have between themselves in private. Tick the items from the list below that they remember to check out.

General area
Bus routes ☐
Local shops, laundrette, etc. ☐

Pubs and other recreational facilities ☐
Is the area relatively safe? ☐

The flat itself
How much is the rent? ☐
How much of a deposit has to be paid? ☐
What are the arrangements for rent collection? ☐
Are there any signs of dampness? ☐
How would you get out in the event of a fire? ☐
Do the windows open? ☐
Is there good ventilation? ☐
Details of arrangements for heating the flat ☐
Are the beds and other items of furniture in
good condition? ☐
Is there enough storage space? ☐
Are all the appliances working? ☐
What are the facilities for washing clothes? ☐
Is there a list of all the items in the flat (an inventory)? ☐
How is the water heated? ☐
How are bills paid? ☐
Who cleans the common areas? ☐
Who else has keys to the flat? ☐
Is the flat hooked up for TV? ☐

Outside
Is there access to the garden and clothes line? ☐
Who takes care of rubbish disposal? ☐
Where can bikes and prams be stored? ☐
Who does the garden? ☐

Rent books and leases

A lease is a verbal or written agreement made between the tenant and the landlord. Because rent books are now required by law, there may be no separate lease. The lease is usually part of and written into the rent book. The primary function of a rent book is to record payments made by the tenant to the landlord, although the following additional information must by law be included:

- The name and address of the rented dwelling.
- The name and address of the landlord or his agent.
- The tenant(s) name.
- The length of the tenancy, which is often one year.
- The amount of rent and how it is to be paid (cash, cheque, standing order, etc.).
- Who is responsible for payments other than rent, e.g. electricity bills, telephone.
- The amount of the deposit and under what circumstances it will be returned.
- An inventory of contents.
- The date the tenancy starts (the date you move in).

In addition to the above it is usually wise to clarify with the landlord each of the following points:

- Under what circumstances can the landlord enter the premises. Ask that he or she does not enter without contacting you first and without you being present.
- An emergency phone number.
- What repairs the landlord is responsible for.

Activity

In a previous activity you looked in your local papers and in estate agencies for three places to let. Imagine you decided to move into one of them. You are now signing the lease. Fill in the sample lease form below. You will have to make up some of the information.

Address of Premises	**Tenancy Details**		
_____	Date of commencement	Day / Month / Year	
_____	Deposit paid	€ _____	
_____	Rent paid in advance	€ _____	
Name and address of Landlord	Term of tenancy (tick one)	Rent	Rent Day
_____	☐ Weekly	€ _____	_____
_____	☐ Monthly	(per week/month)	
_____	☐ Fixed term	From: Day / Month / Year	
_____		To: Day / Month / Year	
Landlord's telephone no. (optional)			

Name and address of landlord's agent (if applicable)	Payment by: (tick one)
_____ _____ _____	Cash ☐ Cheque ☐ Standing order ☐ Landlord's bank and account number (if relevant) _____

Agent's telephone no. (optional)

_____

Account No ☐☐☐☐☐☐☐☐

Deposits are returned at the end of tenancy. Landlords may make reasonable deductions for damage done above normal wear and tear, outstanding bills and/or inadequate notice.

Name(s) of tenant(s)

_____

_____

_____

Payments for services not included in rent

Service	Frequency of payment

(services include electicity, gas, TV, phone, etc.)

Signed _____
        Landlord/Agent

Signed _____
                    Tenants

Tenant and landlord rights and responsibilities

Track 24

Jane has heard so many bad stories about landlords mistreating tenants that she has decided to ring Threshold and get the facts straight. Listen to the conversation on Track 24 and then answer the questions below.

1. Can the landlord increase my rent? _____

_____

2. Does the landlord have to supply me with a rent book?

_____

3. How much notice should the landlord give me if he wants me out?

_____

4. How much notice must I give the landlord if I wish to leave and have not agreed to any fixed period in a lease?

_____

5. If my lease is for a year, can the landlord ask me to leave before the time is up?

_____

6. If I signed a lease for a year and want to leave before the year is up, what risks am I taking?

_____

7. What should I do if my accommodation is in very bad condition?

_____

8. Can the landlord enter the premises whenever he or she chooses?

_____

9. Under what circumstances can the landlord refuse to return my deposit?

_____

10. What are the rules about other people staying in the accommodation?

_____

Running a Home

Activity

Joanne and Mary are sharing a two-bedroom house in Dublin. Both of them are student nurses in a nearby hospital. Make a list of duties or tasks for them and using this list come up with a monthly roster. Make out the roster for them, ensuring that each one does their fair share of work and that the one person is not doing the same job all the time. Some jobs will have to be done every day; others need doing less often.

Sharing with others – potential problems

Activity

Read each of the four problem situations below. Write down the course of action you would take to help solve each of them. Think of other examples and discuss them in small groups.

Situation 1

The landlord collects the rent on a Friday evening at 7 o'clock. One of your flatmates, who is also a good friend, goes to the pub with her workmates on a Friday evening and is never there to pay her share of the rent. You usually end up paying it for her and while she pays you back eventually, you are sometimes stuck for cash between times. It is annoying you.

What should you do?

_____

_____

Situation 2

You live in a house with two other people. For the most part you get along really well. Lately though you have been getting really annoyed when you go to take a bath. There is always a scum around the edge after one of the other two have used it. You always clean the bath until it's spotless so you don't see why you should have to clean it before you get into it as well.

What should you do?

_____

_____

Situation 3

You share a flat with a good friend of yours. Things were going really well until she got herself a new boyfriend. He is never out of the place. You walk into the sitting room to watch TV and there they are cuddling on the couch. They look at you as if you are intruding and make you feel uncomfortable. You now spend most of the evening stuck in your room.

What should you do?

_____

_____

Situation 4

Your flatmate is always using your toiletries and washing powder without asking. Neither of you have much money. You feel unfairly treated.

What should you do?

_____

_____

Key Assignment

For this key assignment you are required to record (either on tape or written) an interview with a young person living away from home. Make up a list of things you feel would be important to ask. You could include some of the questions listed below along with some of your own.

When you have completed this key assignment, go to the beginning of this module and tick it off on the checklist.

1. Would you describe the accommodation that you have at present as good/fair/poor?

2. How much rent do you pay per week?

3. How much on average do you have to spend on essentials every week?

4. What do you see as the main advantage of living away from home?

5. What do you see as the main disadvantage of living away from home?

6. What is your daily routine?

7. What do you do in your free time?

8. Do you find yourself going out to pubs and clubs more or less often now you are not at home?

9. What advice would you give someone thinking of moving out of home?

Exam Time

Social Education (2003) – Long question (part)
1. A rent book is now required by law. List three pieces of information that must be included in a rent book.

1. _____
2. _____
3. _____

2. List **two** sources of information about renting accommodation.

1. _____

2. _____

Social Education (2004) – Long question (part)

2. A. Give **three** pieces of information about **one** of the following types of rented accommodation.

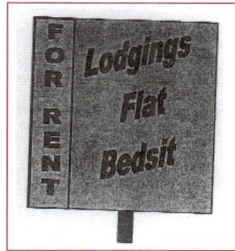

Accommodation:

1. _____

2. _____

3. _____

B. State whether the following statements are true or false.

1. A lease can be an oral or a written agreement. _____

2. A tenant is always entitled to a return of their deposit. _____

3. A tenant is liable for the outstanding rent if s/he leaves before the lease is up. _____

4. A landlord must provide the tenant with a rent book. _____

Unit 2 *Making Ends Meet*

A Balanced Diet on a Budget

Activity

Make up a five-day menu for a young person living away from home. Include breakfast, lunch, an evening meal and a selection of healthy snacks. Make out a shopping list for this five-day menu. Go to the local supermarket and price all the items on the list. What total did you get?

_____

Keep your five-day menu and your shopping list in your Social Education folder as it will be useful for completion of the next key assignment in this unit.

Organising Your Finances

When living away from home it is very important for your health and happiness that essential bills such as rent, electricity, food and gas are paid before you spend money on less essential items such as non-essential clothing and entertainment. Often it is wise to set up direct debit and standing order mandates for these essential bills. Basically what happens is that money for these bills is taken out of your bank account at a specified time each month (or every two months with some household bills, e.g. electricity). Once all essential bills are paid you then have an accurate idea of how much money you have to spend on other things.

Key Assignment

Prepare a weekly budget for a young person living on his or her own. Base this budget on the current weekly wage of a young person who has just started working.

When you have completed this key assignment, go to the beginning of this module and tick it off on the checklist.

Go down to your local job centre, or look in the local papers. Find three jobs advertised that would suit a young person who has just completed their Leaving Certificate Applied.

	Description of Job	**Pay**
Job 1	_____	
Job 2	_____	
Job 3	_____	

Imagine you were to take one of the jobs above. Try to work out a weekly budget based on the wage offered by this job. Below is a list of common expenses incurred by people living out of home. Estimate the average weekly cost of each one. Then see if your budget balances. If it doesn't, you will have to think of ways of making savings.

Clothes _____
Transport _____
Nights out _____
Hobbies _____
Toiletries _____
Cigarettes _____
Breakfasts _____
Work lunches _____
Evening meals _____
Rent _____
Electricity _____
Heating _____
Telephone _____
TV rental _____
Laundry _____
(this could be going to the laundrette or buying washing powder)
Total income = _____
Total expenditure = _____
Balance = _____

Did your income cover your expenditure   Yes ☐   No ☐
If it didn't, where could you make savings?

_____
_____

Activity

You are now in the final year of your Leaving Certificate Applied. Imagine yourself in two to three years' time when you have completed any other courses and have moved out of home. Think about a realistic career that you would like. Find out how much this career pays starting off. Plan a comprehensive and realistic annual budget for yourself.

Activity

Make a list of leisure activities that you could participate in, which cost little or no money.

_____

_____

_____

Exam Time

When living away from home careful budgeting is essential. Give two reasons.

1. _____

2. _____

Unit 3 *Account Options*

Using Cash Only

In the past it was mainly the well off that had bank accounts, chequebooks, etc. The majority of ordinary people operated on a cash-only basis. Their wages were paid in cash and they bought and paid for everything in cash. One good effect of this was that not very many people got into severe debt. You could only spend what you had in your pocket. Having said this, operating on a cash-only basis has its disadvantages. Can you name some of them in the space below?

_____

_____

_____

_____

Key Assignment

Most banks and building societies have an education officer. For this key assignment you must invite the education officer or another official of a bank, building society or credit union to visit your school. Prepare for the visit by making out a list of questions that you would like to ask him or her. Afterwards, report back on what you learned from the visit. Record some of the things you learned below.

When you have completed this key assignment, go to the beginning of this module and tick it off on the checklist.

Five things I learned from the visit are:

_____

_____

_____

_____

_____

The Credit Union

History

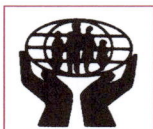

The first credit unions were opened in Ireland in 1958. In the beginning there were only three credit unions in Ireland; today there are over 520 with over 1.8 million members. A credit union is not a building but a group of people who have decided to save together and lend money to each other at reasonable rates of interest. These transactions just take place in the building that you call the credit union. Credit unions are unlike banks or building societies in that members have what is called a common bond. This common bond means that the members of a particular credit union have something between them that unites them. This could be that they all live in the one area; all have the same occupation, e.g. the teachers credit union, or perhaps that all the members belong to a particular society or association.

When you join a credit union, you become one of its owners, and have a say in how it is run. Once you join and pay the usual fee of €1 you are a shareholder and are entitled to vote at the annual general meeting. At the end of the year the profits (called dividends) made by the credit union are divided up among its members. The more shares you have (that is the more you have saved), the bigger the dividend you will receive. When you have been saving with your credit union for a period of time, you can then take out a loan.

Activity

Visit your local credit union and find out the following information.

1. When was this credit union founded?

_____

2. How long do you have to be saving before you can take out a loan?

_____

3. What is the present rate of interest on loans?

_____

4. How long does it take for a decision to be made on your loan?

_____

5. What age do you have to be to join the credit union in your own name?

_____

6. What are the opening hours of this credit union?

_____

7. Apart from savings and lending what other services does this credit union offer?

_____

_____

8. If you have saved €300 how much could you expect to be allowed to borrow?

_____

9. What is the procedure for getting a loan from your credit union?

_____

_____

_____

10. What other advantages are there to being a credit union member as opposed to being a member of a bank?

_____

_____

_____

_____

When you visit your credit union, complete the following forms:

• application for membership   • lodgement form
• loan application form   • withdrawal form.

Although this module requires you to fill in the forms for membership but not necessarily become a member, it might be a good idea to take this opportunity to join your local credit union.

Banking

Nowadays it is becoming more and more necessary to have a bank account. Banks as a result have increased and varied the number of services on offer. In this section we will look at each of the following:

Deposit accounts ☐

Current accounts ☐

Cheque books and cheque cards ☐

Direct debit as a payment method ☐

Standing orders as a payment method ☐

Credit cards ☐

Laser cards ☐

Automated teller machines (ATMs) ☐

24-hour banking ☐

When you have worked through this unit and think you know what each of the above is, tick the box beside it to indicate this.

Deposit accounts

These accounts are also called savings accounts. Although some people use these accounts for all their business they were originally designed for savings, where the account holder would lodge money into the account and leave it there to gather interest. Usually the same forms are used to open deposit accounts and current accounts. An example is given below. All you have to do is tick deposit or current to indicate which type of account you wish to open.

Note: To open an account you will need a photographic ID, for example a passport, and proof of your address.

Activity

Fill out the application form below. It is similar to the form you would be asked to fill out if you wanted to open either a deposit (savings) or current account.

Account required	Savings/deposit ☐	Current ☐

Personal details

Surname _____

First name(s) _____

Address for correspondence _____
_____

Telephone (H) _____ (W) _____

Date of birth _____

Marital status single ☐ married ☐ other ☐

No. of dependent children _____

Do you (Tick one)

Own your home ☐ Rent your home ☐

Live with parents ☐ Other ☐

If you are a student when will you qualify? _____

What course are you studying? _____
_____

Employment details

Occupation _____

Take home pay € _____

Employer's name and address _____
_____

Details of other accounts _____
_____

If you have another account in this bank what is your account number? ☐☐☐☐☐☐☐☐

If you have an account at another bank state the bank and which branch. _____

Do you have any of the following?

Visa ☐ Mastercard ☐ other ☐

Have you a mortgage? Yes ☐ No ☐

If yes, how much is it for? € _____

Signature _____

Date _____

Current accounts

Current accounts are designed to be working accounts. There is no interest paid on current accounts so money does not usually stay in them for long. Most people have a deposit account and a current account. They put spare money into their deposit account and leave it there until they need the money for something special. The current account is for everyday use.

Paying money into your current account

Usually the same form, called a lodgement slip, is used to lodge money into either a current account or a deposit or savings account. All you do is tick the current account box instead.

Activity

Visit your local bank and ask them for two lodgement slips. Fill in each of the slips as follows:

Slip I
Lodge a €144 cheque to your current account. You must make up the account number, the name of the bank and its branch.

Slip 2
Lodge €65 cash to your deposit or savings account. Again make up any numbers, etc. that you may need.

Pay path

In addition to lodging money yourself into your current account, your employer can lodge your wages directly into you current account by what is called 'pay path'. To use this facility your employer will ask you to fill out a form giving your bank details, this form will be sent to your employer's bank, telling them where to lodge your wages every week or month. Sometimes bank loans are easier to get if your wages come in by pay path. Can you think why this should be?

Taking money out of your current account

As a current account is for everyday use so there are many ways in which money can be quickly and easily withdrawn from it. Here are some of the most common methods:

- Cheque book and cheque card
- Direct debit mandates
- Standing orders
- Bank giros
- Laser cards
- 24-hour banking

Cheque book and cheque guarantee cards

If you have a current account, you will probably want to have a chequebook and cheque guarantee card connected with that account. This will allow you to write cheques for goods and services and the money will be removed from your account within a few days. Writing cheques stops you having to carry cash for things like the weekly shop, clothes etc. You would not use a cheque for small purchases as there is a fee imposed for using a cheque. Usually you can only write a cheque up to the amount guaranteed by your cheque card. This is usually about €130. A cheque card guarantees the retailer that the cheque won't 'bounce'.

Activity

You want to purchase a stereo in a local music shop called 'the sound shop'. It costs €79.99. Write out a cheque for that amount. You would have to produce a cheque guarantee card. The retailer or shopkeeper copies down the number of the cheque guarantee card onto the back of the cheque as this would ensure that the cheque will not bounce.

		€
Date _____	Pay _____	91 00 05
Pay _____	_____	euro euro euro
	_____	€ [ ]
Cheque amount _____		Your name
		Signed _____
005438	005438 910005 60000006 07	

Direct debit

A direct debit mandate is an instruction you give your bank to pay out an unfixed amount of money from your account on a regular basis. Electricity bills, phone bills, mortgage payments, etc. can all be paid by direct debit. This means that you will never forget about them and they will be paid on time.

Standing order

A standing order is much like a direct debit mandate except with a standing order the amount paid out is always the same. A standing order could be set up to pay your rent every month. If you were paying fixed amounts for a car over a period of time, you could set up a standing order.

Visit your local bank and ask for a direct debit form and a standing order mandate. Fill each of them for the following:

1. You are forever forgetting to pay your phone bill so you decide to set up a direct debit from your current account (you will have to make up the account numbers, bank and branch).

Can you think of two other bills that could be paid using direct debit?

1._____ 2._____

2. You have taken out an insurance policy on your new car. It was very expensive, so you decided not to pay it all at once but to spread payments over the year. You are required to pay €126 per month. Fill in a standing order mandate instructing your bank to make this payment to your insurance company, which is Smart Drivers Insurance Ltd.

Can you think of two other bills that could be paid using a standing order?

1._____ 2._____

Credit cards

Credit cards allow the cardholder to purchase goods and services up to a certain credit limit using the card. Credit limits usually start at around €750 and then increase, if you show the bank that you can use the card wisely and pay your bills on time. Credit card companies usually give you the option of paying off your bill in full each month or just paying a percentage of what you owe. It is best if you pay your bill off in full each month, so that interest will not be charged on goods or services purchased on the card during that month. The exception to this is if you have withdrawn cash on your card. In this case, interest is charged from the day you withdraw the money.

How a credit card works

When your credit card is swiped through the electronic card reader in, for example, a supermarket, the machine reads the information that is held on the magnetic strip on the back of the card. This strip will hold information such as how much your credit limit is and how much of this limit has been used up. It will also contain information on whether the card has been reported stolen. If you have gone over your limit or are trying to use a stolen card, the electronic card reader will not authorise the sale and you will not be able to purchase the goods.

Some shops have a manual machine as opposed to an electronic one. The shopkeeper must telephone the credit card company to check if the card is OK.

Credit cards can be used in almost every country in the world. They are a valuable asset when travelling abroad. If you ran out of money while on holiday, someone at home could lodge money into your credit card account and you would be able to use your card almost immediately even if you were thousands of miles away. Credit cards can also be used for paying for goods on the internet.

At the end of each month credit card holders get a credit card statement. This statement lists all the purchases made during the month, totals them and states the date to pay by.

Laser cards

Many people who have a current account also have what is called a laser card. This card is swiped through at the cash desk, you sign a receipt and the money is taken out of your current account soon after. Laser cards can be used in many different places such as shops, restaurants and petrol stations. Unlike a credit card, when you use a laser card you are not borrowing on credit but just accessing money already in your bank account.

ATMs

ATM stands for automated teller machine. Common ATMs are Banklink, Pass and Servicetill. Most people use ATMs for one purpose only, which is withdrawing cash. These machines, however, have the capacity to do much more than this, for example you can:

- transfer money between accounts;
- lodge money;
- pay bills;
- get your account balance;
- request a full statement to be sent to you;
- get a mini statement;
- request a new chequebook.

To use these facilities you need an ATM card and a PIN number. (PIN stands for personal identification number.)

Some people have multi-purpose bank cards. One card can be an ATM card, a laser card and a cheque guarantee card all at the same time.

24-Hour banking

ATM machines can be used 24 hours a day, 365 days a year. In addition to this, 24-hour telephone and internet banking now means that a whole range of banking services are available to the public without leaving the comfort of their armchair. If you want to use telephone or internet banking, you will need a security number which you will be asked for before you will be allowed to use any banking services. This is to guarantee the security of your account.

The Post Office

The following financial services are offered at present by the Post Office:

- Prize bonds
- Various deposit or savings accounts;
- Savings bonds
- Money transfer and order service
- Bureau de change
- Instalment savings scheme
- Savings certificates
- Credit card service
- Bill payment service.

Activity

Visit your local post office and find out the following information about the financial services they offer.

1. What are prize bonds?

2. What is the main advantage of prize bonds?

3. Would you consider that investing your money in prize bonds is a good way of saving? Give a reason for your answer.

4. How much money do you need to start buying prize bonds?

5. With the An Post 'instalment savings scheme', how often do you put money into the Post Office?

Every day ☐

Every week ☐

Every month ☐

6. What is the minimum amount that you can invest in each instalment? ☐

7. Would you consider investing your money in this scheme? Give a reason for your answer?

_____

_____

8. What rate of interest does this scheme guarantee if you keep saving for five years or more?

_____

9. Get an application form for a post office deposit account and fill it out. When you have done this tick the box opposite. ☐

10. List two advantages of using the An Post 'pay a bill service'.

_____

_____

11. List six different bills that can be paid using this service.

_____   _____

_____   _____

_____   _____

12. What age do you have to be to get an An Post credit card?

_____

13. What is the Western Union Money Transfer service? Describe what you find out below.

_____

_____

_____

14. What is a bureau de change?

_____

15. Were you surprised at the variety of different services offered by the Post Office?

Yes ☐   No ☐

Building societies

In the past building societies largely concerned themselves with mortgages and investment schemes. As a result of market demands, though, many have expanded their services to include some or all of the following:

- Smaller personal loans
- Insurance – home, life and travel
- Bureau de change
- Pensions
- Savings accounts
- Some have ATM facilities.

Name a building society in your town/area: _____

Activity

Imagine you have €130 to invest. Investigate which institution provides the best investment option.

Institution that provides the best option: _____

Exam Time

Social Education (2002) – Short questions
1. Which of the following dispenses money when you use an authorised card?

ATM ☐   PPP ☐   ERT ☐

2. Which of these services are not provided by the Post Office?

Overdraft ☐   Money Order ☐   Savings Account ☐

Social Education (2003) – Short questions
3. Which of the following accounts has a cheque book?

Current account ☐   Deposit account ☐

Social Education (2004) – Short questions

4. A laser card is used with a:

Current Account ☐   Deposit Account ☐

Fixed Term Account ☐

5. Profits made by the Credit Union are divided amongst its members.

True ☐ False ☐

Social Education (2002) – Long question (part)

6. You are going to buy your first car. You can either get a loan from the Credit Union or from a bank. Give one reason why you might choose a Credit Union loan and one reason why you might choose a bank loan.

A. Credit Union: _____

_____

B. Bank: _____

_____

Social Education (2003) – Long question (part)

7. Outline **two** ways in which the Credit Union differs from other financial institutions.

1. _____

2. _____

8. Explain how **one** of the following cards works:
- Credit card
- Laser card
- Cheque guarantee card

Card name: _____

How it works: _____

_____

Social Education (2004) – Long question (part)

9. Banks offer a wide variety of accounts and services to their customers. These include:
- Cash save account
- Overdraft
- Direct debit

- Term loan
- 24-hour banking

Select **two** of the above and explain how each works.

(1) Account/service _____

How it works _____

_____

(2) Account/service _____

How it works _____

_____

Unit 4 *Saving and Borrowing*

Activity

For this activity, you need to select an expensive item such as a motor bike, CD player, computer, or bicycle, so that you can look at options for acquiring this.

Selected item _____

Price of item _____

There are two options available to you in order to get this item: saving for it or borrowing for it.

Saving

In the previous unit you took a general look at the various financial institutions. For this activity pick three of them, perhaps a bank, the Post Office and a credit union. Find out what rates of interest they offer on savings accounts.

Financial institution	Rate of interest on savings account
_____	_____
_____	_____
_____	_____

When you have found out which financial institution offers the best interest rate, decide how much you can afford to save every week. To do this calculate your average weekly income and your average weekly expenditure and take one from the other.

Weekly saving scheme for purchase of _____

Income	Expenditure
_____	_____
_____	_____
_____	_____
_____	_____
Total _____	Total _____

Total weekly income _____

Total weekly expenditure _____

Balance _____

Number of weeks to save for item _____

Borrowing

Investigate the possibility of getting a loan for the item. If you are under 18 years of age this might prove difficult, but the information may be valuable for the future. The credit union and the bank are the most usual providers of small personal loans. Investigate both of these sources.

Financial institution	Rates of interest of interest	Conditions of approval

Hire purchase

Hire purchase is a form of credit. If you want to buy something and do not have the money for it, you can fill out what is called a credit clearance application form in the shop. The shop then sends this form to the bank. If the bank approves your application, it will pay the shop for the item and you will pay the bank in instalments. Like most forms of credit, the interest rates are usually high and the item will cost you sometimes considerably more than if you paid in full with cash. However, shops sometimes offer interest-free deals in a bid to get your custom. With hire purchase, you have use of the item, but do not officially own it until the last instalment is paid.

Unit 5 *Buying My Own Home*

Mortgages

In the past only building societies offered mortgage loans. Nowadays, that market has widened to include banks, local authorities and life assurance companies. With so many different mortgage packages to choose from, the prospect of getting the right mortgage might seem a bit daunting. Competition of this sort, though, does mean a better deal for the consumer.

Applying for a mortgage

A mortgage is a loan that is given to you to buy property. The property is security for the loan and so you do not technically own your own home until the mortgage is paid in full. There are certain conditions attached to getting a mortgage. You must:

- be over 18 years of age;
- be in secure employment;
- have a sound financial history with no bad debts.

How much can I borrow?

You can borrow no more than 92% of the value of the property you wish to buy. Most mortgage companies nowadays lend at least two and a half times your gross annual salary. If two people are applying, you can add in once the second person's income.

Local authority mortgages

The maximum mortgage given by the local authority (i.e. county council or corporation) is about €42,000. This is likely to increase in the future. Local authority mortgages are similar to other mortgages in that usually you can only borrow up to 92 per cent of the house price and must be 18 years old. In addition you must provide evidence of having been refused a loan from both a bank and a building society. Your income, when multiplied by 2.5, cannot be more than about €45,000.

Compulsory Costs Involved in Buying a House

1. **A deposit**   At least 8% of the house price must be paid.

2. **An indemnity bond**   If you borrow more than 75% of the price of the house, an indemnity bond is often required. Not all organisations have this charge, so it is worth checking this. It is usually between €150-€260.

3. **A surveyor's report**   The building society will send out a surveyor to make sure that the property is worth the money that they are lending to you. You have to meet this cost. It is usually around €150. It is also advised that you get a structural survey done on your property – this survey will point out if there is anything wrong with the property. The cost of this will vary from €150-€400.

4. **Legal fees**   You will have to employ a solicitor, which usually costs 2 per cent of the price of the house.

5. **The solicitor**, in addition to his/her fee, will charge you search fees (€100), land registry (€320), deed registration (€65) and commissioner's fees (€25).
Total = €500 approx.

6. **Stamp duty**   This is a government tax that must be paid on some new and second-hand houses.

Stamp duty (second-hand houses)

Price of house	First-time buyers	Other owner-occupiers
Up to €127,000	0%	0%
€127,000-190,500	0%	3%
€190,501-254,000	0%	4%
€254,001-317,500	0%	5%
€317,501-381,000	3%	6%
€381,001-635,000	6%	7.5%
Over €635,000	9%	9%

Stamp duty (new houses)

- No stamp duty is payable by owner-occupiers on new properties below 125 square metres (1345 sq. ft.).
- The owner-occupier must use the property as their main residence for a period of five years.

- The stamp duty relief will be clawed back if this condition is not followed.
- With new properties larger than 125 square metres, the duty is payable on whichever is the higher of:
  (a) the site cost, or
  (b) 25% of the total cost (site cost + building costs).

Activity

Imagine as a first-time buyer that you are buying a second-hand house with an asking price of €200,000. How much in total will you have to pay? Will you have to pay stamp duty? _____

_____

Some terms explained

Bridging finance/loan A short-term loan to meet the cost of building or buying a new home while the borrower is awaiting the sale of the home he or she already owns. Most people dread this type of loan because of the high rates of interest that are charged.

Mortgage tax relief If you have a mortgage, you are entitled to tax relief on the money you pay in interest. Tax relief is given at source, i.e. by your mortgage lender at the time the mortgage payment is made. This means that your mortgage payment is reduced by the amount of tax relief you are entitled to and your mortgage company then claims this back from the revenue commissioners. For a more detailed account of how mortgage relief works log onto www.revenue.ie .

Home improvement grants Unless you live in a Gaeltacht area and therefore may be entitled to various home improvement grants, there are only a few government grants available. There is:
- A grant available for the repair of a thatched roof.
- An essential repairs grant available to elderly people, who would not be able to remain in their home if these repairs were not carried out.

If, however, you permanently reside in a Gaeltacht area or on one of the islands off our coast and Irish is the main language spoken at home, there are eight different types of grant that may be available to you. For further information on these grants contact the Department of Arts, Heritage, Gaeltacht and the Islands, na Forbacha, Gaillimh.
Tel (091) 592555.

Main Steps Involved in Buying a House

Below is a list of the 12 main steps involved in buying a house. Put the steps in the correct order by putting 1 in the box beside the first step, 2 beside the second step and so on.

Close sale.	_____
Pay fees.	_____
Check newspapers, estate agents ads, sales boards on actual houses.	_____
View properties within your price range.	_____
Employ a solicitor.	_____
Apply for a mortgage.	_____
Put a deposit on the house of your choice.	_____
Employ a surveyor to check the property over.	_____
Sign contracts.	_____
Move in.	_____
Ensure snag list is attended to by builder.	_____
Get mortgage approval.	_____

Activity

Go to a mortgage provider in your area. Ask them to give you details of the mortgage packages they have on offer. Ask them for a mortgage application form. Fill out this form using the following details:

The new house you are buying costs €149,000. You are married and you earn €34,000 per year and your partner earns €32,000.

1. What is the maximum you will be allowed to borrow?

   _____

2. How much money will you have to have for a deposit?

   _____

Invent other likely details for the application form.

Activity

Visit an estate agent's office and/or look in the property pages of local or national newspapers. Research your local housing market. Look at both new and second-hand houses in your area.

Find out the cost of each of:

1. A new, three-bedroom, semi-detached house.

   _____

2. A second-hand, three-bedroom, semi-detached house.

   _____

Exam Time

Social Education (2002) – Short questions
1. A loan to buy a house is called:

   A mortgage ☐   A term loan ☐   An overdraft ☐

Social Education (2003) – Short questions
2. A government tax that must be paid on the purchase of houses over a certain value is called:

   Bridging Finance ☐   Stamp Duty ☐   Home buyers Tax ☐

Social Education (2003) – Long question (part)
3. Fill in the blanks.

   To get a mortgage a person must be _____ years of age. Mortgages can be obtained from _____. You can borrow no more than _____ per cent of the value of the property. Another expense involved in buying a house is _____

Unit 6 *Understanding Insurance*

Some Definitions

Tick off each term if you understand it.

Premium This is the amount of money your insurance policy costs you every year. You pay this to the insurance company. ☐

No-claims bonus You get a discount called a 'no-claims bonus' if you did not have any claims in the last year. With car insurance, to have a full no-claims bonus you need to have had three years' claim-free motoring. ☐

Broker A broker is a person that advises you on what insurance company suits your needs. He or she does not work for one particular insurance company and so will not be pushing one company on you even if it is not the best one for you. He/she is therefore in a position to give unbiased advice. If you take out a policy, the broker takes a commission. ☐

Insurance agent Unlike the broker, the insurance agent sells insurance for one company only, and will therefore be limited to their own product. ☐

Insurance policy This is the name given to the contract between you and the insurance company. It states what is covered, what premium you have to pay, etc. ☐

Renewal notice When your insurance policy is due for renewal, the insurance company will send you a reminder. This is called a renewal notice. ☐

Loadings When an insurance company gets an application for an insurance policy, it assesses that person in terms of risk. If you are a high-risk person, you have a high loading and your insurance will cost more. Young male drivers have a high loading and so can spend well in excess of €2,500 a year on car insurance. ☐

Indemnity This means that you cannot profit from an insurance claim. For example you buy a car for €5,000 and in a year's time when it is only worth €3,800 it is stolen and burned out. You can only claim €3,800, as that is all it was worth at the time. ☐

Types of Insurance

There are various types of insurance that individuals or families may wish to have:

House insurance
This type of insurance covers both the actual building and its contents. In the event of fire or burglary, for example, the insurance company will compensate the owner.

Motor/car insurance
This type of insurance is required by law. Motor insurance can either be third party, third party fire and theft, or comprehensive. Third party means that the damage you do to another person or their vehicle is covered by the policy but not damage to you or your own vehicle. Comprehensive insurance covers you and your own vehicle as well.

Mortgage protection
To get a mortgage you must have this type of insurance. If you have a mortgage and die before paying all of it off, the remainder of the mortgage is paid off by the insurance company.

Private health insurance
You pay a premium to a health insurance company such as VHI or Bupa and, in the event of you becoming ill, you will receive private health care.

Personal accident insurance
This covers you if you had an accident and were unable to work.

Term life insurance
You insure your life for a fixed period of time, for example for 20 years while your children are young and unable to provide for themselves. If you do not die during this period, no compensation is paid out and there is no lump sum at the end of the term.

Assurance

So far we have looked at insurance. Insurance is paying money to a company so that they will compensate you if something happens, e.g. you become ill or have an accident. Assurance, on the other hand, which we will look at briefly now, pays out compensation for something that will happen, for example reaching the age of 65 or dying.

There are two main types of assurance:

Whole-life assurance
The policy holder pays a premium to the insurance company throughout their life. When the policy holder dies, compensation is paid to his or her next of kin.

Endowment life assurance
Compensation is paid out at a fixed age, usually 65. In the event of the policy holder dying before the stated age, the money is paid out then instead.

Activity

You have just bought a four-year-old Toyota Corolla (1.4L). You have recently passed your driving test. This is your first insurance policy. Fill out the motor insurance proposal form below. You will have to invent some details.

Proposal form for Private Motor Insurance

Section 1 - Proposer and Driver details

1. Full Name of Proposer

   _____

   _____

   Address _____

   _____

2. Occupation

   _____

   _____

3. Daytime phone number _____

4. Give details of all persons (including yourself) who will drive the vehicle:

Drivers			Driving Licence Details		
Name	DOB	Occupation	Relationship to you	Full or Provisional	How long is licence held?
Yourself					

		Yes	No	If yes, give details
5.	To the best of your knowledge, have you or anyone else material to this policy ever:			
	(A) Been convicted of an offence or have one pending?	☐	☐	
	(B) Have had any claims against you in the last 5 years?	☐	☐	
	(C) Been disqualified from driving?	☐	☐	
	(D) Have defective vision, diabetes, suffer from fits or heart disease?	☐	☐	
	(E) Been refused insurance by another company?	☐	☐	
6.	Have you or do you hold another insurance policy? If yes, state with which company and its expiry date.	☐	☐	
7.	Are you entitled to a no-claims bonus? (You will have to provide proof of this.)	☐	☐	How many years?
8.	Are you or have you been a named driver on another policy? (If you have proof of this, you may be entitled to a discount.)	☐	☐	How many years?
9.	Who will be the main driver of the car?			
10.	Would you like us to send you information on our house insurance policies?	☐	☐	

Proposal form for Private Motor Insurance

Section 2 - Car details

Reg. No.	Make	Exact model eg. L GI, Turbo, etc.	Cubic Capacity	Year of Manufacture	Present Value	Fuel

	Yes	No	
Is the car owned and registered in your name?	☐	☐	**If 'no' give details**
Is the car right-hand drive?	☐	☐	
Has the car been modified in any way?	☐	☐	**If 'yes' give details**
Will the car be used to pull trailers or caravans?	☐	☐	
Will the car be used for business other than driving to work?	☐	☐	

Declaration:

I _____ confirm that all the details given on this form are to the best of my knowledge true.

Signed _____

Print name _____

Note: Accurate quotes for motor and other forms of insurance are available over the phone.

Activity

Visit an insurance provider in your area. Gather forms, e.g. life, house or mortgage protection insurance. Practise filling the forms.

Note: *How to settle a claim* You must fill out a claim form and send it to your insurance company. The company then sends an assessor to inspect the damage and calculate compensation if it is to be paid.

Exam Time

Social Education (2002) – Long question (part)

1. Study the graph which shows the risk factors involved for motor insurance companies in terms of insuring motorists.

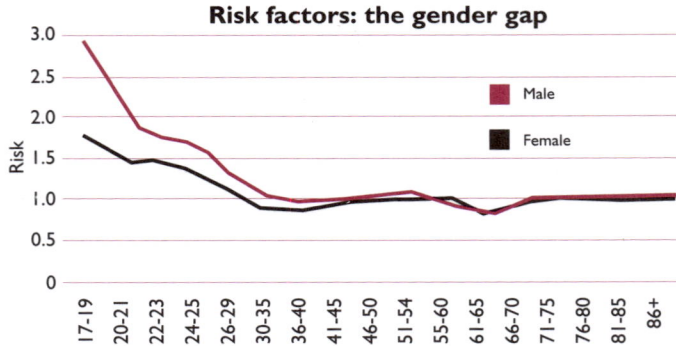

Risk factors: the gender gap

A. Which gender holds the greater risk in the 17-19 age group?

Male ☐   Female ☐

B. Which gender holds the greatest risk in the 24-25 age group?

Male ☐   Female ☐

C. What age group holds the least risk?

41-45 ☐   61-65 ☐   71-75 ☐

D. Do you think that insurance companies treat young drivers fairly?

Yes ☐   No ☐

Give a reason for your answer. _____

_____

2. Explain each of the following terms:

Premium _____

_____

Insurance broker _____

_____

Third party, fire and theft _____

_____